MOOTING AND ADVOCACY SKILLS

MOOTING AND ADVOCACY SKILLS

3rd edition

DAVID POPE
LL.B (Hons.) (Edin.), LL.M (Harvard) of Lincoln's Inn, Barrister
Senior Visiting Fellow, University College London

DAN HILL
MA (Cantab) Head of Learning and Development and
Associate Professor at the University of Law

SWEET & MAXWELL

Published in 2015 by Thomson Reuters (Professional) UK Limited
trading as Sweet & Maxwell, Friars House, 160 Blackfriars Road,
London, SE1 8EZ
(Registered in England & Wales, Company No 1679046.
Registered Office and address for service:
2nd floor, Aldgate House, 33 Aldgate High Street, London EC3N 1DL.)

Typeset by Servis Filmsetting Ltd, Stockport, Cheshire
Printed in Great Britain by Ashford Colour Printers Gosport, Hants

No natural forests were destroyed to make this product;
only farmed timber was used and re-planted.

A CIP catalogue record for this book is available from the British Library

ISBN 9780414037519

Thomson Reuters and the Thomson Reuters logo are trademarks of Thomson Reuters.
Sweet & Maxwell® is a registered trademark of Thomson Reuters (Legal) Limited.

Crown copyright material is reproduced with the permission of the Controller of HMSO
and the Queen's Printer for Scotland.

Contents

APPEARING

David Pope

ORGANISING

Dan Hill

Foreword to the third edition

Judges see advocates differently from the way they see themselves. I have found this one of the most fascinating aspects of making the transition from advocate to judge. As an aspiring advocate, it is always worth bearing in mind.

The call for a third edition of this excellent book is a testament to its success in helping those seeking to make the transition from law student to advocate. I well recall that journey. I was hugely enthusiastic about mooting in those early days and I am sure now that it was that enthusiasm that smoothed my path. Unfortunately, in those dark days, there was no help available. Present-day mooters and moot organisers are fortunate indeed to have access to the down-to-earth guidance in this book.

Readers who pay attention to the authors' wise counsel will be able to avoid the pitfalls that await the ill-prepared mooter. There is nothing more irritating for the mooter or the advocate than an irritable judge. If you follow the meticulous advice to be found in these pages, your submissions will be greeted with nothing but rapt attention. You will never have to experience the judicial tetchiness that my generation of would-be advocates regarded as par for the course.

I heartily recommend the third edition of *Mooting and Advocacy Skills* to all who have an interest in doing mooting properly. It is an excellent, readable *vade mecum*.

Lord Justice Vos

Royal Courts of Justice
London

Biography: David Pope

David Pope is a practising barrister. He was called to the Bar in 1995 and now practises from 3 Stone Buildings, a commercial chancery set of chambers in Lincoln's Inn in London. Before joining 3 Stone Buildings, David was a member of the pioneering advocacy group at global law firm Dentons. He specialises in complex commercial disputes and has acted for multinational banks, Big Four accounting firms, African governments and a Formula One motor racing team, among many others. He appears in the English higher courts as well as international and domestic arbitrations.

David read law at Edinburgh University and Harvard Law School. While at Edinburgh, he was president of its Mooting Society and won the Alexander Stone Scottish Intervarsity Moot Court Competition. He has lectured on mooting to undergraduate and graduate students, and is a Senior Visiting Fellow at University College London, where he teaches a class on advocacy and classical rhetoric.

Biography: Dan Hill

Dan Hill is a solicitor (non-practising) and Associate Professor and Head of Learning and Development at the University of Law. He read social anthropology at Cambridge University and qualified as a solicitor in 1996, specialising in commercial and professional negligence litigation, before joining the College of Law (as it then was) in 2000.

He has extensive experience of teaching and designing programmes at both the academic and vocational stages of training. He set up, and for many years ran, the mooting competition at the University of Law's London, Bloomsbury campus.

He has extensive experience of judging moots and has lectured widely on mooting to undergraduate and graduate students. He was instrumental in establishing the University of Law's LLB and has advised on the preparation of mooting materials for the Institute of Legal Practice and Development in Rwanda, Africa.

Praise for previous editions

"... this is an excellent book for the undergraduate embarking on their first moot, a useful reference for all mooters and a good introduction to advocacy." **Ben Lim, *Solicitors Journal*, 20 March 2011**

"This is an excellent book for anyone who is considering participating in a Mooting Competition or contest, or wishes to learn about the skills needed for mooting. ... I consider this publication a valuable tool for developing mooting skills. Highly recommended." **Dr. Peter Jepson, Head of the Department of Laws, Strode's College, Egham, Surrey**

"It is a very good foundation to both mooting and general advocacy which, essentially, gives the reader confidence to feel that it is not as daunting a topic/skill as perhaps they may have initially thought. ... The thematic approach is totally logical/systematic and very easy/clear to follow. The use of worked examples by way of illustration of the areas covered is excellent. It crystallises the whole thing and certainly assists the reader's understanding greatly." **Wendy Backhouse, Lecturer in Employment Law and Mooting and Advocacy training, Lancashire Law School, University of Central Lancashire**

"This book (Mooting and advocacy skills) is essential for anyone who wishes to take advocacy seriously. I am a 1st year university student and it was highly recommended to me by my university mooting coaches." **Student review, Amazon**

"The book is ideal and highly recommended for those starting out in the world of mooting." ***Review*, mooting.net**

Acknowledgements

I would like to thank Amanda Strange, Senior Publishing Editor at Sweet & Maxwell, for her kind support in bringing this third edition to press. I would also like to thank my wife, Holly Pope, without whose encouragement this book would never have been written.

David

I would like to thank Amanda Strange at Sweet & Maxwell and my wife, Susan Short, for their help and support.

Dan

Preface

Mooting and advocacy have never featured more prominently in British law schools than they do today. Much has changed even in the four years since we wrote the second edition of this book. More universities now offer dedicated mooting modules as part of the law curriculum. Some, including the University of Oxford, have introduced a compulsory mooting element to their undergraduate law degrees. The University of Strathclyde has even launched an entire masters degree devoted to advocacy, the first course of its kind in the UK.

As great believers in the value of mooting, we are delighted by these developments. The augurs are good for more of the same in the coming years. In particular, in 2013, the Legal Education and Training Review published its long-awaited report into legal services education and training regulation in England and Wales. One of the report's key recommendations was that, "greater emphasis should be placed on communication skills". Few law-school activities improve communication skills more effectively than mooting.

As ever more students are drawn into mooting, so the need increases for practical advice on how to moot. Our aim, from the first edition of this book, has been to provide that advice by offering a step-by-step guide to participating in and organising moots. This third edition is no exception. We hope you find that it meets our aim.

London
March 2015

David Pope
Dan Hill

▶ 1
Introduction

This book is principally about mooting. It focuses on the skills of mooting and on organising ▶ 1.1
moots. But the ambit of this book extends beyond the moot courtroom. In the process of
describing how to moot, it provides a toolkit for preparing and delivering persuasive legal arguments. It is therefore intended as a guide not only for those who are involved in mooting
competitions, but also for those who are embarking on professional practice.

    This opening chapter provides an overview of mooting. It poses three questions: what is
a moot, why should you moot and where can you moot? The answers to those questions set
the scene for the remainder of the book. This chapter ends by briefly considering the future of
mooting in Britain.

    Chapters 2–12, which are arranged in two parts entitled "Preparing" and "Appearing",
describe the skills and knowledge that students must acquire to become effective mooters.
These chapters therefore cover, among other things, conducting legal research, drafting
speaking notes and addressing judges correctly. Chapters 13–15 form the final part of this
book, which is entitled "Organising". It looks in detail at how to organise mooting competitions,
explains how to select and write moot problems, and includes several original moot problems.

    Although the primary focus of this book is English law moots, references are regularly
made to the position in Scotland.

WHAT IS A MOOT?

A moot is a simulated appeal court hearing in which law students argue the legal merits of a ▶ 1.2
fictitious civil or criminal case before a mock judge or a panel of mock judges. Moots are not
concerned with the niceties of court procedure or with ascertaining facts. Unlike mock trials,
moots feature neither witnesses nor juries.

    Most moots in the UK, as well as in many Commonwealth jurisdictions, follow a standard
format, which is described in summary below and in greater detail in the remainder of this
book.

Competition rules
Every mooting competition is governed by a unique set of rules. Rules vary widely between ▶ 1.3
competitions. For example, some allow any member of the law student body to participate,
while others restrict entry to undergraduates or novices. Some competition rules require the
participants to draft written arguments in advance of each moot, while others do not. Some

rules lay down a points system that judges must use to decide who wins each moot, while others leave the decision to the judges' discretion. Whatever the precise content of the rules, they should provide the participants with a clear understanding of the competition format. Appendix I contains a specimen set of competition rules.

Participants in moots
Mooters

1.4 ▶ Moots generally involve two teams of two law students. One member of each team acts as "leading" or "senior" counsel and the other assumes the mantle of "junior" counsel. The team members normally decide between themselves who will take which role. In professional practice, junior counsel often say little or nothing during court hearings. Not so in mooting. Leading and junior counsel at moots both make speeches, although leading counsel is typically given more "air time". For that reason, the more experienced mooter, if there is one on the team, tends to act as leading counsel.

One team of mooters represents the fictitious party that lost in the lower court and is appealing against that decision. The other team represents the fictitious party that won in the lower court and wants that decision to be upheld on appeal. In English civil cases, the appealing party is referred to as "the appellant" and the other party as "the respondent". In English criminal cases, the prosecution is always known as "the Crown" and the accused as "the appellant" or "the respondent", as the case may be.

Judges

1.5 ▶ Moot judges simulate the role of judges in real appeal courts. They preside over the moot, listen to the mooters' speeches and give judgment at the end. Moot judges are typically senior law students, law lecturers or practising lawyers. Members of the judiciary—right up to Justices of the Supreme Court—often act as moot judges in the final rounds of big competitions. Most moots feature one judge, but more important moots can involve "benches" of three or even more judges.

Moot court clerks

1.6 ▶ Many moots feature a moot court clerk, who is usually a law student. The moot court clerk's principal task is to time each mooter's speech, but he or she may also perform some of the duties of real court clerks, such as instructing those assembled at the moot to stand when the judge enters the room (customarily with the words, "Court rise") and then announcing the name of the case once everyone is seated. The moot court clerk's role may extend to setting up the moot courtroom and ensuring that the judge has copies of all the relevant documents.

Build-up to moots

1.7 ▶ In advance of the moot, usually one or two weeks beforehand, the teams receive identical copies of a written legal scenario—the moot problem. Among other things, the moot problem describes the factual background that gave rise to the fictitious proceedings, explains the progress of the case to date, summarises the decision of the lower court and lists the grounds of appeal against the lower court's decision. Moot problems are often based on actual reported cases, but with a number of added twists to ensure that the points they raise have not already been decided by the courts.

In the period between receiving the moot problem and the day of the moot, the teams research the legal issues that the problem raises, formulate their arguments and prepare speeches to deliver at the moot. An advocate's arguments, whether written or oral, are commonly known as "submissions". Depending on the competition rules, the teams may have to prepare written submissions—known as "skeleton arguments" in England and Wales—as well as oral submissions. The competition rules also usually require the teams to exchange prior to the moot lists of the "authorities"—the decided cases, textbooks, journal articles and other publications—on which their arguments are based.

Conduct of moots

Moot courtrooms are arranged to resemble real courts. There are consequently designated places for each mooter and for the judge. There is also a seat for the moot court clerk, if there is one, and a public gallery where the audience (usually a motley assortment of students and members of staff) can observe the proceedings. Some law faculties have dedicated moot courtrooms. With their oak-panelled walls and coats of arms above the judges' chairs, these moot courts sometimes look more authentic than the real thing.

▶ 1.8

Once the moot begins, each mooter speaks in a pre-determined order, presenting his or her arguments and responding to the other side's case. Just as in professional practice, the moot judge has the right, which is almost always exercised, to intervene during the mooters' speeches and ask questions. Throughout the proceedings, mooters must observe moot court etiquette.

The competition rules stipulate the speaking time allocated to each mooter. (Hence the need for the court clerk to keep time.) Some mooting competitions ignore the time taken by judicial interventions in computing the period allowed for each mooter's submissions. Others do not. The oral arguments of all the speakers at most moots usually last for a total of about 60–90 minutes.

Conclusion of moots

Once the mooters have completed their oral submissions, the moot judge gives judgment, often after retiring to another room for a few minutes. The judgment consists of two elements: a decision on the law, determining which of the fictitious parties has succeeded on the appeal; and a verdict on the moot, determining which team of mooters has won.[1] Most judges give judgment in that order. Before, or immediately after, announcing who has won the moot, most judges also briefly address what they regard as the strengths and weaknesses of each mooter's performance, and offer some words of wisdom on advocacy technique.

▶ 1.9

Although judges are often guided in their decisions on the moot by specific criteria set out in the competition rules, the winning mooters usually demonstrate the better all-round advocacy skills and the more comprehensive knowledge of the substantive legal issues. It is entirely possible—and, indeed, very common—for the winners of a moot to lose on the law.

---

[1] Occasionally, mooting competition rules provide that the winners of each moot are the two best individual mooters. In those competitions, the judge's verdict on the moot identifies the winning individuals rather than the best team.

WHY SHOULD YOU MOOT?

1.10 ▶ Mooting is hard work. If taken remotely seriously, it involves many hours of trawling through case reports and textbooks, it requires deep thought about complex legal issues and it culminates in a public speech. Yet every year, thousands of British law students moot. Why are these people mooting and, more to the point, why should you join their ranks? Here are seven good reasons.

Mooting makes you think and act like a lawyer

1.11 ▶ Mooting is the closest most students get to practising law while they are at law school. When preparing for and appearing at moots, students must do the very things that most practising lawyers do on a daily basis. They must quickly absorb a set of facts, identify the relevant legal principles and apply those principles to the facts. Not only that, but they must analyse the moot problem from different angles so as to anticipate their opponents' arguments. They must also consider the likely consequences of their own arguments so as to defend them from judges' questions. For practitioners, the ability to analyse legal problems in these ways is essential if they are to represent their clients' interests effectively.

Mooting provides public speaking experience

1.12 ▶ Mooting gives students an opportunity to get up on their feet in public. Any public speaking experience is valuable for students, no matter what they end up doing in their careers. All lawyers, even those who never appear in court, must deliver formal presentations to clients, speeches at conferences and training to their colleagues. So too other professionals: bankers, accountants, teachers, you name it. They must all be able to speak well in public. Mooting is good practice.

Mooting provides advocacy experience

1.13 ▶ Mooting gives students the chance to be advocates. Advocates are not just public speakers. They are persuaders; they persuade judges and juries that their clients should succeed.

Mooting is essential for any student intent on a career as an advocate, whether at the independent Bar, the employed Bar or as a solicitor advocate. But you should also give mooting a go even if you are just toying with the idea of becoming an advocate. The parallels between mooting and real-life advocacy will give you a good indication of whether the life of an advocate really is for you. If so, you may consider more seriously trying to become a practising advocate. If not, far better to find out sooner rather than later.

Mooting helps you learn the law

1.14 ▶ In order to identify and present persuasive arguments at moots, students must obtain a detailed understanding of the legal issues with which the moot problem is concerned. To acquire that understanding, they must hone their research skills beyond the level otherwise required by the legal syllabus. It is not enough for mooters to read a few select passages from a student textbook and scan the headnotes of a couple of cases. Students must read the entirety of a large number of reported decisions, analyse the judgments correctly and work out the ratio of each case.

Since moots tend to raise topical issues in core subjects such as the law of contract and negligence, there is often an overlap with examination questions. As a result, it is a common refrain of students that they remembered the law covered in a moot so well that they did not have to spend much time revising it for their year-end exams.

Mooting gives you confidence

Most students come to mooting with very little experience of the law. Understandably, they often wonder whether they have what it takes to join the ranks of the legal profession. Students who moot gain an enormous amount of confidence in their abilities as lawyers. And why not? If you are able to stand in front of seasoned law tutors or practitioners, even real judges, and persuade them of the merits of your legal arguments, you know that you can cut the mustard.

▶ 1.15

Mooting bolsters your CV

Legal employers are impressed by evidence of mooting on the CVs of job applicants. Participation in mooting demonstrates interest in the practice of law, and commitment to extra-curricular activities. Winning a prestigious mooting competition will make a CV stand out from the crowd.

▶ 1.16

Evidence of mooting is virtually a requirement for the CV of any student applying to become a professional advocate. Advocacy is a relatively small and specialised area of practice. It is consequently a competitive field to break into. There are few better ways for students to demonstrate their interest in and commitment to advocacy than to moot.

Mooting is fun

The vast majority of students enjoy mooting. Like all public speaking, it is genuinely exhilarating. A polished performance, whether on the winning or losing side, will provide a sense of achievement and a "buzz" that few other legal (in every sense of the word) activities can match. But mooting is not just about personal highs. It also has a strong social element, providing an opportunity to get to know members of the teaching staff and the legal profession, as well as fellow students. Just ask Bill and Hillary Clinton. They mooted together when they were students at Yale Law School.

▶ 1.17

WHERE CAN YOU MOOT?

It has never been easier to moot. As little as 25 years ago, mooting was a fringe activity, the province of a few enthusiasts, most of whom had their hearts set on careers at the Bar. Mooting is now mainstream and opportunities abound to moot.

▶ 1.18

Most students moot in the competitions run at their universities. There cannot now be a law school in the country without at least one mooting competition; many offer several, typically a competition for novice mooters and one or more competitions for students who have mooted before. Mooting is an integral part of student life in many institutions, some of which devote considerable space on their websites to mooting.[2]

---

[2]   Among the best university mooting webpages are those of the London School of Economics (*www.lse.ac.uk/collections/law/students/mooting.htm*), Oxford University (*www.law.ox.ac.uk/mooting*) and the University of Aberdeen (*www.abdn.ac.uk/law/student-activities/aberdeen-university-law-mooting-society-96.php*).

For students with a real passion for mooting, the opportunities are almost endless. A host of national inter-institution competitions exists. The leading mooting website, *www.mooting-net.org.uk*, contains a list of these competitions as well as the contact details of the organisers. Some national competitions, including the long-running English-Speaking Union Essex Court Chambers National Mooting Competition, are open to all-comers and cover diverse legal topics. Others are confined to students from law schools in particular geographical areas[3] or to specific areas of the law.[4] Students with an interest in international law can even moot against their peers in other countries. The world's largest mooting competition is the Philip C Jessup International Law Moot Court Competition, which features participants from over 550 law schools in more than 80 countries. Its website lists around 30 other international law mooting competitions.[5]

The plethora of mooting opportunities now available means that students can, if they wish, build substantial mooting "careers". Indeed, it is not unknown for undergraduate students at some British universities to moot more than 50 times. Plenty of professional advocates do not appear in court that often in three years.

THE FUTURE OF MOOTING IN BRITAIN

1.19 ▶ The ever-increasing opportunities for students to moot reflect a trend: mooting is moving from the fringes to the centre of British legal education. That trend is evident in other ways too. The library of mooting literature is burgeoning, for example. More significantly, mooting is creeping into the legal curriculum. Several universities offer dedicated modules on mooting and many others use moots as an aid to teaching academic subjects. In 2007, Alistair Gillespie of De Montfort University and Gary Watt of the University of Warwick produced a report on under-graduate mooting in British law schools.[6] They found that, whereas in 1995 only 20 per cent of institutions offered intra-curricular moots, 59 per cent did so in 2005. That percentage has doubtless risen since. For example, Oxford University recently introduced a mooting unit on its Legal Research & Mooting Skills Programme, which is a compulsory element of its under-graduate law degree.

Even allowing for the recent surge in mooting in Britain, we still lag some way behind Australia, Canada and the USA in making the most of what mooting has to offer. But we are moving in the right direction and will continue to do so in the years to come. After all, mooting suits the zeitgeist. It teaches practical lawyering skills in a problem-based format, yet, by demanding detailed legal knowledge from the participants, it is also highly academic. Most importantly, students demand mooting. They recognise its value. They know that it will improve their legal skills and they know that it will boost their CVs. And what is more, they enjoy it.

---

[3] An example of this type of competition is the London Universities Mooting Shield, which is open to teams of undergraduate law students from universities in London.
[4] For example, the UK Environmental Law Association runs two mooting competitions involving environmental law problems.
[5] See *www.ilsa.org/listings/intlmoots.php*.
[6] Alistair Gillespie & Gary Watt, *Mooting for learning* (2007), which is available at *www.ukcle.ac.uk*.

Preparing

"Preparation is the be-all of good trial work. Everything else—felicity of expression, improvisational brilliance—is a satellite around the sun. Thorough preparation is that sun."

Louis Nizer, US trial lawyer (1902–1994)

Moot problems

Preparation for a moot begins when you receive the moot problem. You cannot start to research the law or to formulate your arguments until you know what the moot is about. The moot problem will tell you.

▶ 2.1

But what do moot problems look like and how should you read them? These are the main questions that this chapter sets out to answer.

WHAT IS A MOOT PROBLEM?

A moot problem describes a hypothetical case in narrative form. Moot problems can be quite lengthy, particularly those used for specialist mooting competitions. For example, the moot problem, or *compromis*, for the Philip C Jessup International Moot Court Competition can exceed 20 pages.

▶ 2.2

Most moot problems set for intra-university mooting competitions are much shorter. Often they are just a single page long and they rarely exceed two pages. Nevertheless, they contain everything the participants need to know about the fictitious case in order to prepare for the moot. In particular, they set out the background facts and the history of the proceedings, and they identify the issues of law that the mooters will argue.

While moot problems raise "live" points of law and usually involve plausible factual scenarios, they are not realistic in the sense that they come without the welter of documents, evidence and client concerns that accompany every legal dispute in professional practice. This lack of realism is quite deliberate. It means that moots can focus on legal arguments without distraction from disputed facts or procedural complications.

THE ILLUSTRATIVE MOOT PROBLEM: *CECIL V DICKENS*

You will understand far more clearly what a moot problem is if you actually see one. Set out in figure 2.1, therefore, is a moot problem entitled *Cecil v Dickens*. It is concerned with the law of negligence and is representative of the type of problem that is commonly used for undergraduate and postgraduate mooting competitions in the UK. In fact, it has been "road tested" in several moots.

▶ 2.3

The text of *Cecil v Dickens* is not provided simply to show you what a moot problem looks like. *Cecil v Dickens* will illustrate many of the mooting skills described later in this book and you may accordingly wish to remind yourself periodically of what it says. Although *Cecil v Dickens* is an English law moot problem, the law of negligence is substantially the same in England and Scotland. The problem should therefore be comprehensible in both jurisdictions.

2.4 ▶ **Figure 2.1:**
Cecil v Dickens

IN THE COURT OF APPEAL (CIVIL DIVISION)

HENRY CECIL

-and-

CHARLES DICKENS

Henry Cecil is a self-employed minicab driver trading as "Cecil and Sons". In January 2007, Cecil and Sons bought "Copperfield Cars", a rival minicab business, for £250,000. Prior to the acquisition, Henry commissioned a report from Wickfield's, a local firm of accountants. Wickfield's advised that it had reviewed the accounts of Copperfield Cars for the previous three accounting periods and that, in view of Copperfield Cars' net profits and assets, the purchase price was reasonable.

In late 2009, it became obvious to Henry that the business of Copperfield Cars was loss-making and that its previous owners had massively overstated its profits and assets. Henry decided to ask his old school friend Charles Dickens for advice. Charles is and was at all relevant times a qualified solicitor practising as "Dickens and Son". In January 2010, Henry met Charles for a drink in a local pub after work. Henry handed Charles the report written by Wickfield's and asked Charles what he (Henry) could do to obtain compensation for the incorrect advice that Wickfield's had given him. Charles listened to Henry's story, took some notes and read through the report. He then said words to the following effect:

> *"Henry, old friend, litigation is not my area of expertise as I specialise in conveyancing, but it is my preliminary view that you have an arguable claim against Wickfield's. Litigation is a risky and expensive business, however, and I suggest that you think carefully about whether or not you wish to sue Wickfield's. If you decide to take matters forward, you should consult a law firm called Barkis & Traddles, which specialises in litigation."*

Henry developed depression a few months after speaking to Charles. He did not contact Barkis & Traddles until the middle of 2013, when he was told that it was no longer possible for him to sue Wickfield's because the relevant six-year limitation period had expired.

Henry subsequently issued proceedings against Charles for negligently failing to advise him that this limitation period would apply to his claim against Wickfield's. At first instance, Mr Justice Steerforth, sitting in the Queen's Bench Division of the High Court of Justice, found in Henry's favour. Mr Justice Steerforth made the following findings:

(A) Even though the relationship between Charles and Henry was social rather than professional, Charles owed a duty of care in negligence to Henry to avoid causing pure economic loss.

(B) Charles breached that duty by not making clear to Henry that a limitation period of six years from the date of acquisition of Copperfield Cars applied to the potential claim against Wickfield's.

(C) Had Charles made it clear to Henry that a limitation period applied to the claim against Wickfield's, Henry would have sought legal advice from Barkis & Traddles before the limitation period expired.

(D) Had Henry sued Wickfield's before the limitation period expired, he would have recovered £100,000. This was accordingly the sum to which Henry was entitled in damages from Charles.

Charles now appeals to the Court of Appeal on the following grounds:

1. No duty of care arose in negligence.
2. If, contrary to the first ground of appeal, a duty of care arose, he did not breach it.

HOW TO READ MOOT PROBLEMS

Like any law-related document, a moot problem should be read with care. Not all of it will sink ▶ 2.5 in first time around, so read it slowly and repeatedly until you are clear about the meaning of every sentence. If the facts are complicated, reproduce them in a comprehensible format as you go along. For example, if the problem involves several inter-related companies, draw a diagram of the group structure so that you can see more easily how they fit together. Similarly, if the problem refers to events that took place at different times, jot down a short chronology so that you are clear about the order in which the events occurred.

Your task in reading moot problems is made slightly easier by the fact that they tend to be arranged according to a standard format. It is described below. There then follows a short list of the main points to note as you read.

Anatomy of moot problems

Most of the moot problems with which you grapple should be laid out much like *Cecil v Dickens*. ▶ 2.6 They will accordingly contain the following elements, typically in the following order:

● Identity of the moot court

The moot problem will identify, usually in the heading, the court in which the moot will take place. In most English law moots, the moot court is the Court of Appeal or the Supreme Court. Scots law moots tend to take place in the Inner House of the Court of Session or the High Court of Justiciary. As you can see from its heading, the moot court in *Cecil v Dickens* is the Civil Division of the Court of Appeal.

● **Identity of the parties**

The heading of the moot problem will also identify the parties, normally in the following order:

- English civil actions: claimant then defendant
- English criminal actions: R (i.e., the Crown) then accused
- Scottish civil actions: pursuer then defender
- Scottish criminal actions: HM Advocate then accused

The moot problem in *Cecil v Dickens* follows this approach, naming the claimant in the proceedings (Mr Cecil) before the defendant (Mr Dickens).

● **Background facts**

The bulk of most moot problems is given over to reciting the factual background of the fictitious case. The facts of a moot problem are sacrosanct. You cannot change or supplement them nor can you invite the judge to do so. In *Cecil v Dickens*, for example, Mr Cecil's case would be strengthened if he had paid Mr Dickens for the advice he received. But there is no mention of payment in the moot problem and the participants must therefore assume that none was made. Nor could the mooters representing Mr Cecil invite the judge to find that Mr Dickens was paid, even in the form of a couple of pints.

● **Procedural history**

Moots are appeals rather than first-instance hearings or trials. Most moot problems therefore include a short explanation of the route that the fictitious case took before it reached the moot court. The route taken by *Cecil v Dickens* is typical of an English moot involving civil proceedings. It began life with a trial before a judge of the High Court and went on appeal to the Civil Division of the Court of Appeal. A different moot problem might feature a case that was further appealed to the Supreme Court. A Scots law moot problem might involve a case that started in the Sheriff Court before being appealed to the Inner House of the Court of Session.

● **Findings of the lower court**

Moot problems almost always contain a synopsis of the lower court's decision. The summary may be short or it may descend to considerable detail, including the authorities on which the lower court relied. The problem in *Cecil v Dickens* includes four findings (paragraphs (A) to (D)) that Mr Justice Steerforth made at first instance.

● **Grounds of appeal**

Moot problems usually end by listing the grounds of appeal. If the grounds of appeal are not stated separately, they will be apparent from the findings of the lower court. The grounds of appeal are the bases on which the decision of the lower court is challenged in the moot (i.e., appeal) court. Most moot problems contain at least two.

Points to note

2.7 ▶ As you read a moot problem, all sorts of thoughts will pop into your head. You may be familiar with the area of law involved and may consequently remember some of the relevant legal principles or recall the names of one or two of the leading cases. You may also find yourself constructing arguments and compiling lists of questions to research. Make notes as you go along. Sometimes the points you spot at this very early stage are among the most insightful. You do not want to forget them.

When you read through any moot problem for the first few times, however, the following issues should be at the forefront of your mind:

● **Place of the moot court in the court hierarchy**

Make an immediate mental note of the moot court. This information is important because the moot court's position in the court hierarchy has a bearing on the weight attached to the decisions you cite as authority. If, for example, the moot court is the English Court of Appeal, you will know that it is bound by any decisions of the Supreme Court, the House of Lords and, save in exceptional circumstances, the Court of Appeal itself.[1]

● **The party you represent**

Ensure that you know from the word go which party you represent. You might think that it will be blindingly obvious from the moot problem, but sometimes it is not. Take *Cecil v Dickens*. In accordance with the usual practice for English civil actions explained above, the heading of the illustrative moot problem names the parties in the order claimant then defendant. But Mr Cecil's claim succeeded at first instance and it is Mr Dickens who has appealed. Mr Dickens is therefore the appellant in the moot and Mr Cecil is the respondent. If you were told that you were acting for the appellant, you would accordingly be representing Mr Dickens, even though his name appears second in the heading of the problem. If you are in any doubt about which party you represent, check with the moot organiser. It is far better to ask what might seem like a silly question than to join the ranks of mooters—and there are many out there—who have researched a problem on behalf of the wrong party.

● **Relevance of each fact**

As you read through the section of the moot problem that describes the factual background, ask yourself continually whether you understand the legal significance of each given fact. Although some moot problem authors are more prone than others to embellishing their work with irrelevant background information, virtually all of the facts in a well-drafted moot problem assist one or other of the parties. The facts will therefore help you to identify the arguments that you and your opponents should run. For example, the moot problem in *Cecil v Dickens* states that Mr Dickens advised Mr Cecil in a local pub after work. This fact suggests that the advice was provided in a social, rather than a business, setting. It is relevant because the English courts rarely find duties of care to avoid pure economic loss in social situations. The fact therefore helps Mr Dickens.

● **Reasoning of the lower court**

Pay particular attention to the summary of the lower court's findings. The reasoning of the judge below usually forms the basis for the respondent's submissions. It is therefore a launch

---

[1] Ch. 3 explains the court hierarchies in England and Wales, and in Scotland.

pad for both parties' legal research, all the more so if it identifies a key authority or two on which the lower court relied. The lower court's findings may also clarify the scope of the matters in issue at the moot. For example, paragraphs (C) and (D) of the lower court's findings in *Cecil v Dickens* are concerned with whether Mr Dickens's alleged breach of duty caused Mr Cecil to suffer loss and, if so, the amount of damages to which Mr Cecil is entitled. Since Mr Dickens is not appealing against either of those findings, the moot is not concerned with issues of causation and loss.

● Scope of the grounds of appeal

In similar fashion to appeals before real courts, you must usually confine your arguments at moots to the grounds of appeal specified in the moot problem. There are only two grounds of appeal in *Cecil v Dickens*. The first is concerned with the circumstances in which duties of care to avoid pure economic loss arise in negligence, specifically when advice is given in a social situation. The second ground of appeal is concerned with the standard of care that applies if a duty of care exists and whether it was breached in this case. The parties would consequently address their arguments to those issues and those issues only. Counsel for Mr Cecil could not argue, for example, that there was a contract between the parties under which Mr Dickens ought to be liable.

DISCUSSING THE MOOT PROBLEM WITH YOUR TEAM-MATE

2.8 ▶ If you are part of a team, discuss the moot problem with your mooting partner shortly after you receive it. A conversation with your team-mate at the outset will help you to identify the relevant issues. Your partner may have spotted points that you did not and vice versa. Some of those points may be good, others not so. By debating them, you should produce some useful initial ideas and prevent a few diversionary hares from running. Your discussion should include a consideration of the overall merits of the moot problem. Do you or your opponents have the better case? What are your weaknesses? What are theirs?

Another reason for having an early discussion with your team-mate is that you can use it to work out how best to divide the legal research between you. Come the moot, you will need to be reasonably conversant with each other's submissions in case the judge asks one of you a question about an issue that the other intends to cover. It is nonetheless unlikely to be a sensible use of time for both of you to research all of the same ground in detail.

Very often, the moot problem presents a clear way of splitting the work. In *Cecil v Dickens*, for example, there are two grounds of appeal. Since the second ground of appeal logically depends on the first (i.e., if there is no duty of care, it cannot have been breached), the obvious division of labour is for the team member who will speak first to research the first ground of appeal and for the other team member to take the second ground of appeal. The former will then research duty of care, while the latter researches standards of care and breach.

If the moot problem does not present a clear division of labour, you and your team-mate may have to begin your researches independently. This approach should not result in too much duplication if it is confined to the early stages of research. Keep the position constantly under review, however. As and when an appropriate allocation of work becomes apparent, divide up the research along those lines.

WHEN YOU HAVE THE WEAKER CASE

However well crafted a moot problem may be, the legal merits will always favour one side more than the other. For example, as the law of England currently stands, the problem of *Cecil v Dickens* favours the appellant, Mr Dickens. When giving judgment on the law (as opposed to a verdict on the best mooters), a judge presiding over a moot employing this problem should therefore decide to uphold the appeal. ▶ 2.9

There may be times when you read a moot problem and form the view that the merits are against you. But even if you are right, the weakness of your legal case is not a bar to you winning the moot. On the contrary, having the weaker case has certain advantages. In particular, the judge will probably have a good idea of where the legal merits lie and will give credit for fighting an uphill battle effectively. Mooters defending weak legal positions will therefore win plaudits for any reasonable argument they present. They may even be forgiven the odd poor submission on the grounds that the fund of helpful material was limited.

For these reasons, some seasoned mooters prefer to have the weaker case in law. At any rate, being in that position should be no cause for alarm.

CHAPTER CHECKLIST

- ● Read the moot problem carefully several times. ▶ 2.10
- ● Note the court in which the moot will take place.
- ● Ensure you know which party you represent.
- ● Try to work out the legal significance of every fact in the moot problem.
- ● If the facts of the moot problem are complicated, reproduce them in the form of a diagram or chronology.
- ● Identify the precise scope of the grounds of appeal.
- ● Discuss the moot problem with your team-mate (if you have one) to allocate work and discuss first impressions.
- ● Do not worry if you appear to have the weaker legal case.

▶ 3
Legal research

3.1 ▶ If your experience of courtroom advocacy is limited to watching TV dramas, you could be forgiven for thinking that winning a legal argument is all about grandstanding in court. But as any practising advocate will tell you, it is the "hard yards" spent researching the case and constructing arguments that underpin success at hearings. Precisely the same principle applies in mooting.

This chapter examines the skills required to conduct research for moots.[1] It begins by discussing the ultimate objective of research—persuasive arguments. It then describes the research process, separating it into four phases. After looking at a worked example using the illustrative case of *Cecil v Dickens*, the chapter ends with a short description of the principal sources of research material.

THE ULTIMATE OBJECTIVE: PERSUASIVE ARGUMENTS

3.2 ▶ A moot is a debate about the law and you will take sides in that debate. The ultimate objective of your research is therefore to furnish you with the arguments that you will present in your oral submissions at the moot and in any written skeleton argument that you draft in advance. Those arguments must cover both your positive and negative cases. Your positive case consists of the reasons why you say that the fictitious party you represent should succeed on the law. If you act for the appellant (or the reclaimer in certain Scottish moots[2]), your positive case is therefore the arguments that support each ground of appeal. If you represent the respondent, your positive case is the arguments that demonstrate why each ground of appeal should fail. Whichever party you represent, your negative case is the reasons why you say that your opponents' submissions should fail.

Whether part of your positive or negative case, each of your arguments should help to persuade the judge that your side ought to win the moot. But what makes an argument persuasive? That question is considered next.

Means of persuasion

3.3 ▶ The ancient Greeks were fascinated by the persuasive impact that particular modes of writing and speaking had on audiences. They developed a complex field of study known as rhetoric

---

[1] This chapter is not, however, a comprehensive guide to conducting legal research. If you need broader assistance with your research skills, you might consult *Knowles, Effective Legal Research*, 3rd edn (2012), another book in the same series as this text.

[2] In Scotland, a party appealing from the Outer House of the Court of Session to the Inner House is known as "the reclaimer" rather than "the appellant".

that sought to explain the phenomenon. The leading figure of Greek rhetoric was the philosopher Aristotle. He discovered that persuasive speakers use the following three means of persuasion:

● *Ethos*

A speaker's *ēthos* is his or her credibility with the audience. Aristotle realised that audiences believe some people more than others. Speakers with high levels of credibility are significantly more persuasive than those with limited credibility.

● *Pathos*

Pathos refers to the emotions of the audience. As Aristotle put it, things do not seem the same to people in different emotional states; an angry audience and a contented audience react differently to the same speech. The accomplished speaker understands the audience's emotions and is able to influence them.

● *Logos*

The Ancient Greek word *logos* literally means "what is said". In a rhetorical context, *logos* refers to the reasoning inherent in an argument. A well-reasoned speech is more persuasive than a speech containing logical flaws. As a man of reason, Aristotle wanted people to be persuaded by *logos* alone. But he recognised that certain weaknesses in mankind's make-up render us susceptible to the baser appeals of *ēthos* and *pathos*. He therefore advised speakers to use those appeals, in addition to *logos*, to sway audiences.

Means of persuasion in mooting

Aristotle's advice holds good in mooting. Effective moot-court advocates deploy all three means of persuasion. You might wonder how *ēthos* enters a moot. You will certainly not bolster your credentials by explaining how well you did in previous moots or by saying that you passed your last tort law exam with flying colours, and no eminent reputation precedes your performance. Nonetheless, you can enhance your credibility by "looking the part", both in the way you dress and in the way you act. If you wear a suit, you will score points over a team that turns up in scruff order.[3] If you produce an immaculate skeleton argument, free of typos, spelling mistakes and grammatical errors, you will also give the judge an impression of competence and boost your credibility.[4] In a close moot, these *ēthos* factors can make a difference.

> 3.4

    Pathos also comes into play in mooting. Skilled mooters actively try to establish an "emotional connection" with the judge. Through regular eye contact, appropriate gesturing and professional demeanour, a rapport can be developed that provides an added edge. *Pathos* can work the other way too. While it may seem obvious, you must avoid angering the judge. Be aware that some judges in moot courts and real courts take personally what they regard as disrespect. Examples include advocates who interrupt the judge's questions or fail to turn off their mobile phones. Raising a negative emotion in the judge will only present you with another obstacle to overcome.

---

[3]   Ch. 9 explains how students should dress for moots.
[4]   Ch. 4 considers the importance of good spelling, grammar and punctuation in moot skeleton arguments, and describes some of the most common mistakes of English usage that mooters make.

While *ēthos* and *pathos* therefore play their parts in persuading moot judges, the most important means of persuasion in mooting is *logos*. Moot judges, in common with professional judges, are persuaded first and foremost by sound legal reasoning.

Forms of legal reasoning

3.5 ▶ According to Aristotle (and no-one has seriously challenged him in nearly 2,500 years), all reasoning is either deductive or inductive. A persuasive legal argument is therefore founded on valid deductive or inductive reasoning.

Deductive reasoning

3.6 ▶ Deductive reasoning draws conclusions from the application of valid general rules (major premises) to specific situations (minor premises). Deductive arguments are known as syllogisms. The following argument is a syllogism:

Major premise: All mooters are law students
Minor premise: Sally is a mooter
Conclusion: Sally is a law student

Deductive reasoning underpins all legal arguments in rule-based systems of law (as the English and Scottish legal systems are). It establishes a link between a legal rule of general application and the facts of the case at hand so as to arrive at a particular conclusion. The basic building blocks of deductive legal arguments for moots are therefore as follows:

Major premise: Generally-applicable legal rule
Minor premise: Relevant facts of the moot problem
Conclusion: Decision that the moot court should make

Lawyers and mooters derive legal rules for the major premises of their deductive arguments from recognised "authorities". Authorities include decided cases, textbooks, articles in legal journals and, in Scotland, certain works of the so-called institutional writers.

You will see when you read reported cases that many judgments closely resemble extended syllogisms. In particular, they often contain a review of the relevant authorities from which an applicable legal rule (the major premise) is drawn and then "apply" the rule to the facts of the case (the minor premise) to reach a conclusion. An especially clear example of this approach is the judgment of Neuberger J (now Lord Neuberger) in *Money Markets International Stockbrokers Ltd v London Stock Exchange Ltd*,[5] in which the judge explained as follows how he intended to proceed:

> "... I shall start by discussing the authorities, and shall then turn to consider the principles to be derived from the cases. I shall then seek to apply those principles to the present case."[6]

Deductive legal arguments will feature in both your positive and negative cases at a moot. In order to build a positive deductive argument, you will search the relevant authorities

---

[5] Money Markets International Stockbrokers Ltd v London Stock Exchange Ltd [2002] 1 W.L.R. 1150.
[6] [2002] 1 W.L.R. 1150, 1163C.

for a principle of law that will act as your major premise. You will then apply that rule to what you identify as the critical facts of the moot problem to reach the desired conclusion. In order to build a negative deductive argument, you will attack the major and minor premises of your opponents' arguments. You will, in other words, look for ways to dispute the validity of the legal rules that your opponents have drawn from their authorities (their major premises) and argue that those rules, even if valid, do not apply to the facts of the moot problem (their minor premises). If you succeed, you will break the logical thread of your opponents' arguments and render their conclusions invalid.

Inductive reasoning

Inductive reasoning draws conclusions from particular instances. Inductive legal argument takes two forms. The first form—known as synthesis—derives conclusions from multiple instances. In criminal trials, for example, the prosecution often relies on several pieces of circumstantial evidence to reach the conclusion that the accused is guilty. Similarly, mooters regularly argue in favour of particular legal rules that they have synthesised from multiple sources. A mooter might, for example, argue that a legal rule can be derived from a statutory provision and two decided cases that interpret it.   ▶ 3.7

The second form of inductive legal argument—known as analogy—draws conclusions from single instances. In legal argument, the single instance is typically a decided case. In common law systems subject to the doctrine of precedent, previous court decisions are accorded respect so as to ensure wherever possible that similar cases are treated alike. Using analogical reasoning, a mooter might argue that the facts of the moot problem are so similar to those of a helpful decided case that the judge should "follow" the earlier decision at the moot. Conversely, a mooter might argue that an unhelpful decision should not be followed because it is different in material respects from the moot problem. The mooter would conclude such an argument by asking the judge to "distinguish" the earlier case.

OVERVIEW OF THE RESEARCH PROCESS

So, you know the ultimate objective of your research, but how do you get there? How do you generate persuasive arguments? There is no single route. Different people conduct research for moots equally successfully using different methods. Nonetheless, it is possible to sketch out a basic model. The model comprises the following four phases: ▶ 3.8

● **Phase 1: understand the legal context**
During this phase, which follows a careful reading of the moot problem,[7] you obtain an understanding of the relevant legal backdrop. This phase is a relatively short, but important, step in the research process.

● **Phase 2: conduct detailed research**
Phase 2 is when you carry out your in-depth research into each of the grounds of appeal. It is usually the longest phase of the research process.

---

[7]   Ch. 2 explains how to read moot problems.

● **Phase 3: finalise arguments and select authorities**

This phase covers the period before you serve your list of authorities and draft any skeleton argument. During it, you finalise the arguments that make up your positive case and select the authorities that your side will cite at the moot.

● **Phase 4: refute your opponents' case**

The final phase begins when you receive your opponents' list of authorities and any skeleton argument. It lasts until the moot begins. Most of this phase is spent coming up with ways to refute your opponents' arguments.

No claim is made here that each of these phases can or should form a distinct, hermetically sealed component of the research process. On the contrary, there will inevitably be significant overlaps between them. For the sake of convenience, however, each phase is considered separately below.

PHASE 1: UNDERSTAND THE LEGAL CONTEXT

3.9 ▶ It is essential that, from the very beginning of the research process, you understand the general principles of law that govern the legal issues with which the moot problem is concerned. If you appreciate the legal context, you will find it far easier to read and make the most of the authorities that you come across during your in-depth research. The benefits of a "helicopter view" go farther than that, however. Moot problems, by definition, raise unresolved legal issues. In order to reach decisions on those issues, moot judges are usually forced to fall back on first principles. The arguments that you develop must be consistent with those principles. You therefore need to know what they are.

Where to find the general principles

3.10 ▶ The best place to look for an overview of the general principles of any particular area of law is usually the leading practitioner textbook in the field.[8] Practitioner textbooks are ideally suited to this purpose. They focus on "black letter" law, describing the law as it is, not as it should be. They are also accurate, detailed and up to date.

If you are unable to lay your hands on the relevant practitioner text, you have two main options. The first is to read the relevant pages of a good student textbook. Compared to practitioner textbooks, student texts are more discursive and less detail-oriented, and they tend to be updated less frequently. You should therefore ensure that any student textbooks you read were published recently. On the credit side of the ledger, student textbooks are normally more readily available to mooters because law libraries often stock multiple copies and many students possess copies themselves. In addition, the layout and writing styles of student texts are more accessible than those of practitioner textbooks, and mooters may accordingly find them easier to use.

Your second option is to read the relevant paragraphs of *Halsbury's Laws of England* (for an English law moot) or *The Laws of Scotland: Stair Memorial Encyclopaedia* (for a Scots

---

[8] Tables 3.6 and 3.7 below list some of the leading English law and Scots law practitioner textbooks in several key disciplines.

law moot). Neither publication descends to the detail of most practitioner, or even student, textbooks, but both should offer accurate and up-to-date summaries of the guiding legal principles.

Practical considerations

Whichever source you plunder for your understanding of the legal context, you will inevitably come across references to potentially important authorities. Start to compile a running list of these authorities for use later in the research process. This list will help to ensure that you do not overlook a critical case or text.

▶ 3.11

Although obtaining an understanding of the context is a vital part of the research process, you are likely to find that it becomes increasingly abbreviated as your legal experience grows. As a young undergraduate preparing for your first moot, you may be completely unfamiliar with the relevant area of law. This phase of the research process will then take up a significant amount of your time. By contrast, as a seasoned postgraduate student studying for your vocational exams, you should have a decent grasp of most of the topics that habitually crop up in moots. This phase may then involve little more than reading a few pages of a tried and trusted textbook, and jotting down a handful of references to authority.

PHASE 2: CONDUCT DETAILED RESEARCH

Once you have an overview of the general legal principles under your belt, you can start your detailed research. This phase of the research process essentially consists of a hunt for the most relevant and important authorities. It involves three broad elements: identifying potentially relevant authorities; deciding which authorities are sufficiently important to read; and reading those authorities.

▶ 3.12

How to identify relevant authorities

You will find potentially relevant authorities by scouring the sources available to you. The principal sources of authorities are described at the end of this chapter. They include case reports, textbooks and journal articles. You will probably search through most of these sources online. Whenever you come across a reference to an authority of potential interest, add it to the running list that you started to compile during the first phase of your research.

▶ 3.13

The process of tracking down authorities should resemble an investigation. A footnote in a textbook may lead you to a reported decision that, in turn, refers to another, more helpful, case. If you come to feel a little like a private detective, so much the better.

How to decide which authorities to read

If you are thorough, your running list of potentially relevant authorities will grow quickly. Most of the authorities on your list will be case reports. A few of these cases will immediately stand out as particularly significant and you will probably read them the moment you discover them. Since you are unlikely to have sufficient time to read every one of the remaining cases on your list, you will have to develop a system of triage for identifying the most important.

▶ 3.14

Your ability to separate the wheat from the chaff will improve with experience. But what if you lack that experience? Set out below are four pointers to assist you in eliminating cases of tangential relevance:

● **Concentrate on the cases that crop up most often**
If you find that a particular case is mentioned time and again, it is probably one of the more important ones and is therefore worth reading.

● **Make full use of headnotes**
Almost every reported case, even those available online, includes a headnote that briefly summarises the facts, the procedural history and the findings of the court. The headnote should provide you with a good indication of whether the case is relevant for your purposes. If that indication is clearly negative, it makes little sense to read the entire report.

● **Read the most recent decisions first**
If you uncover several cases that address a particular legal issue, read the most recently decided first. It may summarise the earlier cases for you and save you the trouble of reading them. It may also refer to cases that are more "on point" and therefore of potentially greater use to you. You can then make a beeline for them.

● **Do not read first instance decisions of cases that went to appeal**
When the lower court and appeal court decisions of a particular case are both reported, you can generally confine yourself to reading the latter. Some series of law reports helpfully set out next to each other the speeches of both the lower and appeal courts. If the judgments of different courts in a single set of proceedings are reported separately, however, you must ensure that you read the decision of the higher court. It is a sobering experience to wade through a seemingly significant judgment only to find that it was subsequently overturned on appeal.

How to read authorities

3.15 ▶ Once you have identified the most important authorities, you need to read them. Thoroughly. Case reports, in particular, require careful attention. If you fail to read an important decided case from beginning to end, you may miss some useful material such as a helpful quote or case reference. Worse still, you may pick up the wrong end of the stick: in your haste, you might misunderstand a critical part of the judgment and believe it to support your case when it actually goes against you; or you might read a dissenting or differing judgment and mistakenly take it to represent the views of the majority of the court. These sorts of mistakes can land you in a lot of hot water, particularly if the realisation that you have misread a case only dawns on you at the moot.

As you read authorities, look to extract from them material that will help to bolster the arguments you have already thought of and to identify further, possibly more persuasive, arguments. Those tasks are usually pretty straightforward when you read textbooks and articles because authors tend to articulate their points in an argumentative way. Drawing material from decided cases can be more complicated. When reading them, you should have your eyes peeled, in particular, for the following:

● **Helpful statements of legal principle**

Top of your wish list are clear statements of the law that support your case. What you are looking for is that core sentence or two in which the judge explains what the law is. You will quickly develop a facility for spotting these passages. You must ensure, however, that the helpful excerpt is of general application and is not expressly limited to the facts of the particular case.

● **The judge's reasoning**

Judgments, like arguments, are based on reasoning. You must work out how the judge reached his or her conclusion. Judges usually explain their thought processes before setting out their conclusions. You may be able to use the same chain of reasoning in one of your arguments.

● **Arguments of counsel**

Judges often refer in their judgments to the arguments that counsel advanced before them. Some series of law reports even summarise counsel's principal submissions just after the headnote. These summaries can be fertile ground because you can often adapt counsel's arguments for your own purposes. But be careful, when reading judgments, not to confuse the judges' summaries of counsel's arguments with the judges' findings. Judges sometimes refer to counsel's arguments only to reject them.

PHASE 3: FINALISE ARGUMENTS AND SELECT AUTHORITIES

Throughout the research process, you must think about possible arguments. During the early phases of your research, concentrate on your positive case. You should, of course, give *some* thought to identifying the thrust of the case that your opponents are likely to make and to considering how you will meet it. If you do so, you will be better placed to refute your opponents' case in detail when you exchange lists of authorities and any skeleton arguments. Generally speaking, however, it is unwise to focus too heavily on your negative case until you exchange with the other side because your efforts will be wasted if your opponents take a different tack from the one you were expecting.

▶ 3.16

As the moot draws nearer, you must decide on the arguments that will make up your positive case and fine-tune them. If you have to serve a skeleton argument in advance of the moot, you will need to settle on the points that appear in it. Even if no skeleton is required, you will have to work out which authorities to cite at the moot. Since those authorities will support your arguments, you need to know which arguments you will run.

Most mooting competitions limit the number of authorities that each side can cite, sometimes to as few as three. Even if you are free from such a restriction, there is bound to be a time limit on your oral submissions. It will act as an effective constraint on the number of authorities that your team cites because you will simply have insufficient time in which to take the judge through more than a handful.

The next few pages provide a few pointers that you should bear in mind when deciding which authorities to cite.

Select the most weighty authorities

3.17 ▶ As a general rule, choose the authorities that carry the greatest legal weight. The two factors described below largely determine "weight" in this sense.

Type of authority

3.18 ▶ Different types of authority have different weights. Figure 3.1 shows, in very broad terms, the "pecking order" of English authorities.

3.19 ▶

Figure 3.1:
Hierarchy of English authorities

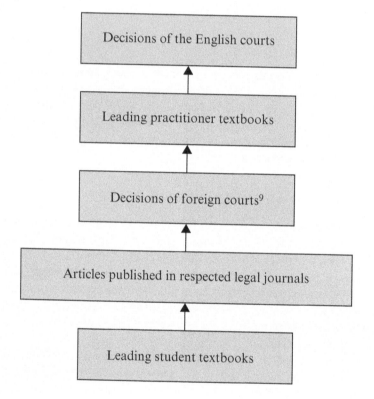

In Scotland, the "pecking order" is much the same, except that the institutional writings provide an additional form of authority broadly on a par with decisions of the higher Scottish courts.[10]

Most, if not all, of the authorities you cite should come from the top of the hierarchy in figure 3.1. Your list of authorities should usually therefore consist of the names of several

---

[9] The most authoritative jurisdictions for English law purposes are Australia, Canada, New Zealand, the United States and (for contract and tort law in particular) Scotland.
[10] The most authoritative foreign jurisdictions also differ. The Scottish mooter may, for example, gain assistance from decisions of the South African courts.

decided cases from your own jurisdiction. There may be exceptions, however. For example, when the principles of a particular area of law are not set out in a single case, but are scattered across many, you might cite as one of your authorities a respected practitioner textbook that summarises the relevant law rather than cite one reported decision that only provides a partial picture. The moot judge may ask you to justify your choice of authority, but will probably view favourably your explanation that you were constrained by the number of authorities you could cite.

Level of court
The top band of the hierarchy of authorities in figure 3.1 (decisions of the English courts) is itself subject to a further "pecking order". The weight of a decision depends on the position in the court hierarchy of the court that made it. The court hierarchy in England and Wales is shown in simplistic terms in figure 3.2. The court structure in Scotland is rather different. It is illustrated in figure 3.3.

▶ 3.20

▶ 3.21

Figure 3.2:
Hierarchy of courts in England and Wales

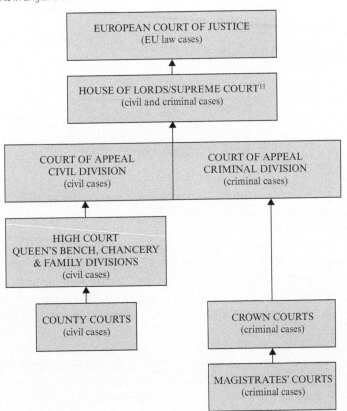

3.22 ▶

Figure 3.3:
Hierarchy of courts in Scotland

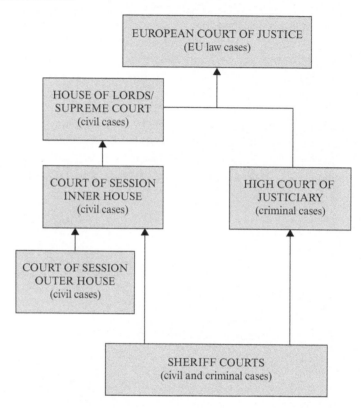

The decisions of any given court bind the courts below it in these hierarchies. A decision of the Civil Division of the English Court of Appeal therefore binds the English High Court, County Courts, Crown Courts and Magistrates' Courts.

Most courts are not bound by their own decisions although those decisions are highly persuasive. This principle applies to the Supreme Court, albeit that it will presumably follow the practice of the House of Lords and only very rarely depart from its earlier decisions. The exception to this rule is the English Court of Appeal, which is bound by its own decisions save in the exceptional circumstances enumerated in *Young v Bristol Aeroplane Co Ltd*.[12]

Select the most recently decided cases

3.23 ▶ When you find yourself with two or more reported cases of roughly equivalent legal weight, you should generally cite the most modern decision. You might even cite a recent case in preference to an earlier decision made by a court higher up the court hierarchy if the recent case contains a comprehensive summary of the present state of the law or of the way in which the

---

[12] [1944] K.B. 718.

law has developed. The modern tendency of judges to produce lengthy judgments means that you are quite often presented in a single speech not only with a helpful recitation of the relevant legal principles, but with a smörgåsbord of excerpts from the leading cases. By citing an authority such as this, you can show the moot judge the most important passages in a number of other cases. But there are limits to how far you can take this approach without infringing the rules of most mooting competitions. In particular, you cannot normally cite a case that refers to other authorities and then seek to introduce material about those other authorities that does not appear in the case you cited.

Be wary of dissenting or differing judgments

As a general rule, only cite a case in order to rely on the views expressed by the majority of the court. That is not to say that you should never rely on a minority judgment. A dissenting judge may, for example, disagree only on the facts, his or her reasoning on the law being consistent with the remainder of the court. You may then safely use that reasoning to bolster your case. You might also cite a minority judgment of a particularly distinguished member of the judiciary whose dissenting view is now taken to represent the law. But you need to be careful, particularly if the speeches of the majority of the court are unhelpful to your case and can consequently be relied on by your opponents.

▷ 3.24

For similar reasons, be wary of relying on the words of judges who, although in the majority in upholding or rejecting an appeal, reached their decisions for different reasons. The reasoning of the differing judges may not assist you even if the result of the case does.

Do not cite unhelpful authorities

Mooters acting on behalf of appellants are particularly prone to the affliction of citing cases that were decided against them. Their rationale is usually that, because they will address the moot court first, they will be able to "rubbish" the authority before their opponents get to their feet.

▷ 3.25

Citing authorities in this way is almost always a mistake. If the authority is genuinely helpful to your opponents, they will probably cite it themselves, in which case you can address it when you refute their arguments during your oral submissions. If your opponents do not cite the authority and you do, you will needlessly present them with additional ammunition.

Less is more

Citing more authorities does not guarantee a better argument. On the contrary, mooters often cite far too many authorities and, as a result, do not do full justice to any of them. In most moots, it should be perfectly possible to rely on one or two authorities per ground of appeal.

▷ 3.26

If you are satisfied that you have enough authorities of sufficient weight to make good the arguments that you intend to advance at the moot, there is nothing to be gained from citing further, makeweight authorities simply because you can. Nor should you indulge in the tiresome sport of deliberately citing off-beam (and usually lengthy) cases in the hope of sending your opponents on a wild-goose chase. Even if your opponents take the bait, the judge or the moot organiser will probably spot the attempted deception. They will not be impressed.

PHASE 4: REFUTE YOUR OPPONENTS' CASE

3.27 ▶ The final phase of the research process begins when you receive your opponents' list of authorities and any skeleton argument that they have drafted, and lasts until the start of the moot. During this period, the primary focus of your research is usually your negative case, that is to say the refutation of your opponents' arguments.[13] If they have served a skeleton, it should tell you explicitly what those arguments are. Even if you only see a list of authorities, you should be able to work out fairly accurately what your opponents will say. In any event, you must read carefully each of the authorities on which your opponents rely.

Analyse your opponents' case with the same logical rigour that you brought to bear in constructing your positive arguments. Concentrate in particular on the major and minor premises of their arguments. Have your opponents correctly identified the relevant legal rules (major premises)? If so, have they correctly applied those rules to the relevant facts of the moot problem (minor premises)? More specifically, look to refute your opponents' arguments on the lines described below.

Your opponents' authorities do not represent the law

3.28 ▶ You may be able to argue that an authority cited by your opponents does not reflect the current state of the law. For example, a reported case may be inconsistent with another decision made by a court higher up the court hierarchy. You may even be lucky enough to find that one of your opponents' authorities has been expressly doubted, criticised or not followed in a subsequent case.

More rarely, you might notice that your opponents are relying on a case that was decided without reference to an inconsistent *earlier* authority that the court ought to have taken into account. Decisions of this sort are said to have been made *per incuriam* (literally, "through lack of care"). They arise most often in relatively lowly courts where counsel and judges are more prone to overlook existing case law.

Your opponents have misread their authorities

3.29 ▶ You may accept that a reported case cited by your opponents was correctly decided, but still argue that they have drawn the wrong principle from it. You might notice, for example, that your opponents are hanging their hats on a passage in a judgment that does not reflect the decision the court made; other parts of the same judgment may be inconsistent with it or the judge may have been in the minority of a multi-member tribunal. Similarly, you may find that your opponents are relying on statements that are mere obiter dicta and form no part of the ratio of the decision. These passages are of limited weight and may readily be "trumped" by other authorities.

Your opponents' authorities are distinguishable

3.30 ▶ Even if you accept that an authority cited by your opponents correctly sets out a relevant legal rule, you may be able to contend that it does not apply to the moot problem. Judges sometimes

---

[13] At the same time, of course, you will be drafting the notes that you take with you to the moot and practising your oral submissions. You may also be preparing copies of your authorities for the judge. These topics are discussed in Chs 5–7.

state that their findings of law should be limited to the particular facts of the cases before them. Statements of this type are manna from heaven if you are attempting to distinguish an unhelpful decision. Even if your opponents' authority is not expressly limited in this way, its facts will inevitably differ in one or more material respects from the facts of the moot problem. A difference in fact is material in this sense if it would have altered the court's reasoning in some way.

Your opponents' arguments are contrary to policy

Your opponents may be running an argument that, if accepted by the court, could have unpal- ▶ 3.31
atable consequences in future cases. If so, you can submit that the argument should be rejected as a matter of policy.

Arguments based on supposed policy considerations are often the last resort of the desperate mooter. They are not without their uses, however, particularly if the policy alluded to has been expounded frequently by the courts. An example is the oft-expressed policy of the English courts that novel categories of negligence should only develop incrementally and by analogy with established categories.[14] In a moot concerned with the law of negligence, you might be able to contend that your opponents' argument falls foul of this policy because it would result in a significant extension of the categories of negligence.

Another common policy argument, which is of more general application, goes something like this: if the court allows your opponents to succeed in this particular case, it will open the floodgates to a deluge of similar claims by other litigants. This point can be powerful. But if you use it as part of your refutation, be ready to explain *precisely* why the floodgates would open if the court were to accept your opponents' argument.

TAKING EFFECTIVE NOTES

Throughout the four phases of the research process described above, you should take compre- ▶ 3.32
hensive and comprehensible notes. Much of the effort expended in conducting your research will be wasted if your notes are so poor that you cannot rely on, or even understand, them when you come to prepare your oral submissions and any skeleton argument.

It is particularly important that you make effective notes about the leading cases that you uncover. Unless you are blessed with an elephantine memory, you will find that the details of even the most factually gripping cases slip from your mind very soon after you read them.

To be of most use to you, your notes on key reported cases should include at least the following information:

● The citation

Head your notes for each case with the full case name and law report citation (or citations if the case appears in more than one series of law reports). A complete and accurate citation will enable you to find the authority quickly in future.

---

[14]   This policy is referred to, for example, by Lord Bridge of Harwich in *Caparo Industries plc v Dickman* [1990] 2 A.C. 605, 618.

● **The court in which the case was decided**

This information will help you to work out the relative importance of the cases that you find and, in particular, to know whether the moot court is bound by them.

● **A summary of the principal facts**

You can usually keep this section short. Make a note of the central facts and any unusual or amusing features of the case that may help to jog your memory. Descend to greater detail if you believe that you are likely to cite the case at the moot.

● **A synopsis of the court's reasoning**

Identify briefly the point or points of law that the court considered, the decision that it reached and its main reasons for doing so.

● **Important references**

Note the page or paragraph references of the most important passages of each judgment. You may have to find these passages again before the moot and you will not want to re-read the entire report to do so.

FIVE COMMON MISTAKES

3.33 ▶ There are plenty of mistakes to be made when conducting research for moots. The purpose of this section is to identify five of the most common errors that mooters make and to suggest how you can avoid them.

Underestimating the time that research takes

3.34 ▶ Mooters routinely fail to appreciate just how long it takes to research a moot problem properly. The issues that moot problems raise have often been pondered long and hard by legions of senior lawyers and judges. It is consequently no mean feat for a student to get to grips with them. Do not be surprised, therefore, if your researches take far longer to complete than you anticipated when you first read the moot problem.

Believing that there is a solution to the moot problem

3.35 ▶ Some mooters think that, if they search diligently enough, they will find a reported case that comprehensively determines the law in their favour. Do not fall into this trap. The notion that there is a "solution" to the problem is inconsistent with the nature and purpose of mooting. Moot problems are designed to have no clear answer. Indeed, the availability of arguable points for both sides is essential if the moot problem is to bring out the best in all of the participants.

This feature of moot problems means that you should not treat your research as a quest for a single decided case. During the course of your labours, you may, of course, find a case on which the moot problem appears to have been modelled. But there will always be some way of distinguishing that case, whether on the basis that there are important differences in the central facts or that there are other reported cases that cast doubt on its correctness.[15]

---

[15] For a sense of how moot problems are normally written, see Ch. 14.

Failing to see the wood for the trees

One of the most enjoyable aspects of researching the law for moots is tracking down authorities—the investigative element referred to earlier in this chapter. But mooters must make the most of the limited research time at their disposal. Little will be gained, for example, from detailed research into the historical origins of legal principles. Nor will there be any material benefit in protracted research into the case law of distant jurisdictions with no track record of influencing the courts of this country.   ▌3.36

Whilst it is perfectly sensible to follow leads, even if initially unpromising, you should take stock from time to time. Ask yourself what your research is uncovering, whether you will be able to use any of this material at the moot and whether your research is preventing you from investigating more promising avenues. If your efforts are proving largely unproductive, you will probably make better use of your time by following a different line of enquiry.

Failing to see the wood for the paper

As your research progresses, supplement your notes with hard copies of the leading authorities. You will then have a permanent record of your research and be protected from the risk that your source material is not available the next time you head to the law library.   ▌3.37

Keep your copying under control, however. You should not usually reproduce whole chapters of textbooks nor do you need to obtain copies of every case report you read. If you take that course, you will quickly find yourself suffocated by a mass of paper, relatively little of which will provide any real assistance.

Failing to work as a team

If you have a mooting partner, do not work in isolation. Instead, meet as often as you reasonably can to discuss the progress that you are making with your research. Regular get-togethers will provide an opportunity to work through any difficulties that you encounter. Very often, the best way of finding solutions to legal problems is to explain them to someone else. Sometimes, the "problem" then reveals itself not to be an issue at all. On other occasions, the act of describing the problem brings forth a means of dealing with it. You may even find that your partner comes up with an elegant solution. And if all else fails, and the problem remains intractable, at least you have a shoulder to cry on.   ▌3.38

A WORKED EXAMPLE

The research skills described in this chapter may be illuminated by a short example. Set out below, therefore, is a description of how you might go about researching the first ground of appeal in the illustrative moot problem of *Cecil v Dickens* if you were acting on behalf of the appellant, Mr Dickens. Needless to say, the process described here is a much-abridged version of what you would actually do in practice.   ▌3.39

The text of *Cecil v Dickens* appears in full in Ch. 2. The first ground of appeal states that, "No duty of care arose in negligence". As counsel for the appellant, your objective would be to build a case in support of that statement.

Phase 1: understand the legal context

3.40 As you would realise on your first read through the moot problem, the broad issue brought into play by the first ground of appeal in *Cecil v Dickens* is the existence of a duty of care in negligence. The first phase of your research would accordingly focus on understanding what a duty of care is and the principles that determine when a duty of care arises.

Following the advice given earlier in this chapter, you might look for this understanding in the leading English law practitioner textbook on tort, which is *Clerk & Lindsell on Torts*.[16] Negligence is discussed in Ch. 8, with duty of care examined at paras 8.05–8.120. Many of these paragraphs are irrelevant for your purpose, however, and could accordingly be skipped. In fact, the relevant sections only run to around 40 pages. They would provide an excellent grounding in the principles that govern the existence of duties of care in negligence including the various tests that the courts apply.

You would also see that para. 8.120 of *Clerk & Lindsell* contains a discussion about the specific issue raised by the first ground of appeal in *Cecil v Dickens*, namely whether a duty of care to avoid economic loss can arise when the relationship between the parties is social. That paragraph identifies two reported cases in which this issue was specifically considered: *Spring v Guardian Assurance plc* (*Spring*)[17] and *Chaudhry v Prabhakar* (*Chaudhry*).[18] These cases could form the beginnings of your running list of potentially relevant authorities.

Phase 2: conduct detailed research

3.41 The second phase of the research process might begin with a search for cases other than *Spring* and *Chaudhry* in which the English courts have considered whether a duty of care to avoid pure economic loss can arise in social situations. You would find very little, however, so you might next research in detail the general principles that govern the existence of duties of care when a person's negligence causes pure economic loss. There is an enormous amount of material on this topic. You would find, in particular, that the House of Lords reviewed the relevant principles in *Customs and Excise Commissioners v Barclays Bank plc* (*Barclays*).[19] You would therefore add this case to your running list.

At some point during your detailed research, you would read the *Spring*, *Chaudhry* and *Barclays* decisions. You would discover as follows:

- In *Spring*, the House of Lords held that an employer who gives a reference to a former employee owes a duty of care in its preparation. However, two members of the House of Lords (Lords Slynn and Woolf) doubted whether the giver of a reference to a social acquaintance would owe a duty of care. This case is therefore broadly helpful to your side of the argument.
- In *Chaudhry*, the Court of Appeal held that the defendant, who advised a family friend about buying a second-hand car, *did* owe a duty of care. This case is therefore broadly unhelpful to your side of the argument, but highly relevant because your opponents should cite it as one of their authorities.

---

16 Table 3.6 lists the leading English law practitioner texts in seven subject areas including tort.
17 [1995] 2 A.C. 296.
18 [1989] 1 W.L.R. 29.
19 [2006] UKHL 28; [2007] 1 A.C. 181.

● In *Barclays*, the House of Lords used the following three tests to determine whether a duty of care arose to avoid pure economic loss: (1) whether the defendant had "assumed responsibility" for the claimant; (2) whether the so-called "three-fold" test applied in *Caparo Industries plc v Dickman* (*Caparo*)[20] had been satisfied (i.e., the loss was foreseeable, there was a relationship of proximity between the parties and it was fair, just and reasonable to impose a duty); and (3) whether the imposition of a duty of care would be "incremental" to previous cases. This decision is important because it illustrates the approach that the courts now take when deciding whether to impose a duty of care in financial loss cases.

You would find that these decisions refer to several reported cases that would be worth adding to your running list and, in due course, reading. They include *Caparo, Hedley Byrne & Co Ltd v Heller & Partners Ltd* (*Hedley Byrne*)[21] and *White v Jones.*[22] Your detailed research might range in other directions too. The judgments in *Barclays* refer, for example, to three separate articles in the *Law Quarterly Review*. You might find some interesting material in them. You might also spend some time looking for relevant case law from overseas. Australia and New Zealand are particularly fertile sources of jurisprudence about negligence.

Phase 3: finalise arguments and select authorities

Whilst reading the material that you unearthed during your detailed research, you would start to formulate arguments. There are numerous arguments available to both sides in *Cecil v Dickens*. By way of illustration, figure 3.4 summarises one possible line of argument for the appellant's positive case.[23] This line of argument uses deductive reasoning. It applies the rules set out in *Barclays* (the major premise) to particular facts of the moot problem (the minor premise).

▶ 3.42

Having settled on a line of argument, you would need to draw up your list of authorities. Were you to employ the argument summarised in figure 3.4, your most important authority would be *Barclays*. As a decision of the House of Lords, it binds the moot court. It is also of relatively recent vintage. If you were only able to select one authority, this case might well be it. With more authorities to play with, you might also consider citing *Spring* and paragraph 8.120 of *Clerk & Lindsell*.

Phase 4: refute your opponents' case

The arguments you came up with to refute your opponents' case would depend on the authorities that they cited. If their research had been as careful as yours, however, it is safe to assume that their list of authorities would include *Chaudhry*. In the last phase of the research process, you would therefore look for ways to undermine that decision. Figure 3.5 lists two of the arguments open to you.

▶ 3.43

[20] [1990] 2 A.C. 605.
[21] [1964] A.C. 465.
[22] [1995] A.C. 207.
[23] This line of argument provides the basis for part of the sample skeleton argument included in Ch. 4.

These arguments use inductive—specifically analogical—reasoning. They compare *Chaudhry* with the moot problem and identify material differences between the two cases. The conclusion of these arguments would be that the moot judge should distinguish *Chaudhry*.

3.44 ▶   **Figure 3.4:**
Possible line of argument

- The leading case is *Barclays*.
- None of the tests applied by the House of Lords in *Barclays* is satisfied in this case for the following reasons:

  – The fact that Mr Dickens told Mr Cecil that he should consult litigation solicitors if he decided to pursue a claim against the accountants shows that Mr Dickens did not "assume responsibility" for Mr Cecil.
  – It was not reasonably foreseeable that Mr Cecil would wait for more than three years after speaking to Mr Dickens before he contacted litigation solicitors.
  – It would not be fair, just and reasonable to impose a duty of care on Mr Dickens given the social context in which he advised Mr Cecil. The context includes the friendship between the parties and the fact that the advice was given in a pub.

- The imposition of a duty of care would not be "incremental" because *Cecil v Dickens* is quite different from other cases in which the courts have imposed duties of care to avoid pure economic loss, e.g., where an employer gave a reference to an employee (*Spring*) and where a solicitor failed to draft a will (*White v Jones*).

3.45 ▶   **Figure 3.5:**
Possible basis for refutation

- The two judges in *Chaudhry* who held that a duty of care existed (Lord Justices Stocker and Stuart-Smith) were heavily influenced by the fact that there was a relationship of agent and principal between the parties. No such relationship exists in *Cecil v Dickens*.
- The facts of *Chaudhry* were very different from *Cecil v Dickens*. For example, whereas in *Chaudhry*, the defendant told the claimant not to seek advice from anyone else, Mr Dickens specifically told Mr Cecil to consult litigation solicitors if he wanted to proceed with a claim against the accountants.

PRIMARY SOURCES FOR RESEARCH

3.46 ▶   This final section of the chapter describes the primary sources of information that you are likely to use when conducting research for moots. If you are to make the most of those resources, you will need to hone your online and paper-based research skills.

Case reports

Case reports contain the full text of judgments in significant decided cases as well as a head-note for each decision. In the more authoritative series of law reports, including the *Law Reports* and the *Weekly Law Reports* in England, and *Session Cases* in Scotland, the authorities referred to in the judgments of the court are listed at the beginning of each report. The *Law Reports* and the *Weekly Law Reports* even go so far as to list the cases that counsel cited in argument, but that are not referred to in the judgments. ▶ 3.47

In addition to being high-level authorities themselves, decided cases are a vital source of information about other authorities. Many higher court judgments, in particular, contain scholarly examinations of the law that refer not only to previously decided cases, both at home and abroad, but also to academic commentary in textbooks and journal articles.

Practitioner textbooks

Practitioner textbooks are primarily aimed at the legal profession and are usually written by prominent practising lawyers or academics. They refer, sometimes at considerable length, to the leading decided cases and are often laden with lengthy footnotes containing references to reported cases and seminal journal articles. ▶ 3.48

Tables 3.6 and 3.7 list by subject area some of the most well-known English law and Scots law practitioner textbooks. These lists are not definitive. In many areas of the law, other excellent practitioner textbooks exist that you may find just as useful.

Table 3.6: ▶ 3.49
English law practitioner textbooks

Subject area	Textbook	Current edition
Company law	*Gore-Browne on Companies*	Looseleaf
Contract law	*Chitty on Contracts*	31st (2012)
Criminal law	*Archbold*	New edition annually
Equity and trusts	*Snell's Equity*	32nd (2013)
Land law	*Emmet and Farrand on Title*	Looseleaf
Private international law	*Dicey, Morris & Collins on the Conflict of Laws*	15th (2012)
Tort law	*Clerk & Lindsell on Torts*	20th (2013)

Table 3.7: ▶ 3.50
Scots law practitioner textbooks

Subject area	Textbook	Current edition
Company law	*Gore-Browne on Companies*	Looseleaf
Contract law	*McBryde, The Law of Contract in Scotland*	3rd (2007)
Criminal law	*Gordon, The Criminal Law of Scotland*	3rd (2010)
Delict	*Walker, Delict*	2nd (1981)
Land law	*Gordon and Wortley, Scottish Land Law*	3rd (2009)
Private international law	*Anton's Private International Law*	3rd (2011)
Trusts and succession	*Meston, Scottish Trusts and Succession Service*	Looseleaf

Halsbury's Laws/The Stair Memorial Encyclopaedia

3.51 ▶ *Halsbury's Laws of England* and *The Laws of Scotland: Stair Memorial Encyclopaedia* are encyclopaedias of English and Scots law respectively. The latest, fifth edition of *Halsbury's Laws* will run to 101 volumes, not including indices and supplements, and *The Stair Memorial Encyclopaedia* fills 25 volumes.

Since the range of *Halsbury's Laws* and *The Stair Memorial Encyclopaedia* is far wider than any individual textbook, you must search them effectively for information. It is beyond the scope of this work to explain how to conduct such a search, but there are several guides on the subject if you require assistance.[24]

Journal articles

3.52 ▶ There is a bewildering array of legal journals and periodicals available to law students. They range from overtly academic publications like the *Law Quarterly Review* and the *Modern Law Review* to specialist practitioner periodicals such as *Computers & Law* and the *Journal of International Banking Law and Regulation*.

The focus of most journal articles is very narrow, often a single decided case or a technical legal issue. As a result, reading journals should not form a major component of your legal research for moots. If you have the time, however, a quick, targeted search for potentially relevant articles can bear fruit. In particular, well-researched articles can provide useful ideas for arguments and point you in the direction of decided cases that other sources miss, especially decisions of foreign courts.

Student textbooks

3.53 ▶ The best textbooks aimed at undergraduates contain accurate, accessible and reasonably full descriptions of the law. They also refer to all of the important reported cases. Although it is not easy to identify the pre-eminent student texts, it is probably safe to rely on any textbook that your tutors recommend for a particular subject.

Lecture notes and handouts

3.54 ▶ Do not underestimate your lecture notes and handouts as sources of relevant authorities. Any law tutors worth their salt will ensure that the materials they produce refer to the latest legal developments.

Legal dictionaries

3.55 ▶ Some moot problems are concerned with the meanings of particular words or phrases. If you are faced with a moot problem of this sort, look up one or more of the leading legal dictionaries, in addition to a conventional dictionary. The best-known English legal dictionaries are probably *Stroud's Judicial Dictionary of Words and Phrases*[25] and *Words and Phrases Legally Defined*.[26] Both include references to reported cases in which the meanings of the defined words and phrases were considered.

---

[24] For guidance on searching *Halsbury's Laws*, both in print and online, see *Knowles, Effective Legal Research, 3rd edn (2012)*, pp.114-118.
[25] 8th edn (2013).
[26] 4th edn (2007).

Online sources

Many of the sources described above are available online. Although some databases can be accessed free of charge, the most comprehensive, and therefore the most useful for research purposes, are available only to subscribers. If you are a student at a law faculty in the UK, chances are that you will have access through the university's subscription.

▶ 3.56

Web-based sources of legal information were virtually non-existent 15 years ago and the materials available online are increasing year-on-year. At present, however, the three most commonly available British commercial databases are probably Westlaw UK, LexisNexis and Lawtel. The key features of each are described briefly below. For a more detailed explanation both of what these databases contain and how to use them effectively, consult a specialist text.[27]

● Westlaw UK

Westlaw UK provides access to UK case law and legislation as well as journals published by Sweet & Maxwell. Its case coverage extends to over 100 series of law reports including the *Law Reports* and the *Weekly Law Reports*. Westlaw UK also contains a comprehensive collection of EU case law, including judgments handed down by the European Court of Justice and the European Court of First Instance.

● LexisNexis

LexisNexis provides access to a range of databases covering, among other things, UK and EU case reports, UK legislation and legal journals published by Butterworths. It also includes a number of practitioner textbooks and *Halsbury's Laws*.

● Lawtel

Lawtel is used principally by practitioners. Its great virtue is that it is updated daily with the most recent, often as yet unreported, court decisions. It therefore provides the very latest intelligence about the law. However, unlike Westlaw UK and LexisNexis, Lawtel does not contain links to any series of law reports.

In addition to the subscription services described above, several free databases provide access to case law and legislation. Two prime examples are the website of the British and Irish Legal Information Institute (*www.bailii.org*), which draws together publicly available transcripts of recent decisions of certain English and Scottish courts (among others), and *www.legislation.gov.uk*, which contains the full texts of all primary and delegated legislation enacted by the UK Parliament since 1988 and most pre-1988 primary legislation.

CHAPTER CHECKLIST

- Read the relevant passages of a leading practitioner textbook to gain an understanding of the general legal principles pertaining to the area of law with which the moot problem is concerned.

▶ 3.57

---

[27] See, for example, *Knowles, Effective Legal Research*, 3rd edn (2012), at pp.8-24.

- Keep a running list of all potentially useful authorities.
- Identify the most important authorities, read them thoroughly and make effective notes about them.
- Constantly review your progress and abandon any unproductive lines of inquiry.
- Do not look for the "solution" to the moot problem.
- Look instead for arguments that use valid deductive and inductive reasoning.
- Only cite authorities with significant legal weight.
- Never underestimate how long your research will take.

▶ 4
Skeleton arguments

Reflecting the widespread use of written advocacy in modern British courts, many UK mooting competitions require the participants to produce skeleton arguments.[1] The ability to draft a persuasive skeleton argument is therefore a key skill for the modern mooter.

> ▶ 4.1

This chapter begins by explaining what a skeleton argument is. With the assistance of examples using the illustrative case of *Cecil v Dickens*, it then describes in detail what skeleton arguments should contain and how to go about drafting them.

WHAT IS A SKELETON ARGUMENT?

A skeleton argument is a written outline of a party's case. It should introduce the judge to the issues that arise for determination at the moot and summarise briefly, but persuasively, all of the main arguments that your team intends to advance. It should also refer to each of the authorities on which your team relies. The English Court of Appeal has enumerated the functions that good skeleton arguments perform as follows:

> ▶ 4.2

> "... an agenda for the hearing, a summary of the main points, propositions and arguments to be developed orally, a useful way of noting citations and references, a convenient place for making cross-references, a time-saving means of avoiding unnecessary dictation to the court and laborious and pointless note-taking by the court."[2]

This description applies as much to moot skeleton arguments as to those in professional practice.

Rise of skeleton arguments

The increasing prevalence of skeleton arguments in moots reflects their growing importance in professional practice, particularly in the civil courts. Gone are the days when a judge's introduction to a case came when counsel rose to their feet at the beginning of the hearing. Now, skeleton arguments are mandatory in England and Wales for all but the shortest of procedural hearings.

> ▶ 4.3

There are two main reasons for the burgeoning use of skeleton arguments in practice. The first is that skeletons enable judges to prepare more effectively for hearings. Since

---

[1]   The term "skeleton argument" is used throughout this book for ease of reference. It derives from professional practice in England and Wales. In Scotland, written submissions tend to be called "notes of argument".

[2]   *Raja v Van Hoogstraten* [2008] EWCA Civ 1444; [2009] 1 W.L.R. 1143, 1172 per Mummery LJ.

advocates must serve their skeletons on the court (and on each other) in advance of hearings, judges know beforehand what their cases are about and can identify the issues on which to focus when the advocates are on their feet. The second reason is that skeleton arguments promote fairness between the parties. Both sides know in advance what the other will say and no-one is ambushed at the hearing. The advocates' oral submissions can then concentrate on the real issues in dispute.

Rules on skeleton arguments

4.4 ▶ The procedural rules of the British courts impose varied requirements for the format and service of skeleton arguments. In the English Admiralty and Commercial Courts, for example, skeleton arguments for trials must be no more than 50 pages long, claimants must serve their skeletons at least two clear days before the trial begins and defendants must serve theirs at least one clear day before trial.[3]

Likewise, the rules of any mooting competition in which skeleton arguments are mandatory will impose certain requirements. Typically, skeleton arguments are subject to a page or word limit and each side is obliged to exchange its skeleton with the other side ahead of the moot (usually 24 or 48 hours beforehand). In a bid to prevent mooters and judges from being taken by surprise, the rules of some mooting competitions also require the participants to identify in their skeletons—if only in broad terms—every argument that they intend to raise in oral submissions at the moot. Unless you wish to attract the ire of the judge, and potentially lose marks, you must abide by these rules.

Arrangement of skeleton arguments

4.5 ▶ There is a well-recognised basic arrangement for skeleton arguments. It applies as much to a 50-page skeleton drafted by counsel for a major court hearing as it does to a one-page skeleton prepared for the first round of a mooting competition. That layout appears in figure 4.1.

4.6 ▶ **Figure 4.1:**
Basic layout of skeleton arguments

HEADING (including the parties and the court)

INTRODUCTION

SUBMISSIONS (i.e., arguments)

CONCLUDING PARAGRAPH

Names of counsel

Date

---

[3] The Admiralty and Commercial Courts Guide, paras J6.2 and J6.5.

The template in figure 4.1 consists of four principal elements: the heading; the introduction; the submissions; and the conclusion. Each of these elements is considered in turn below.

HEADING

The heading of your skeleton argument should enable the reader, particularly the judge, to identify quickly what the document is and the fictitious party on whose behalf it has been served. For English law moots, you should ideally adopt the form of heading illustrated by figure 4.2. It is a simplified version of the standard heading used by professional lawyers in England and Wales. It does not take up much space, so you should be able to use it even if your skeleton argument is subject to a tight page or word limit.

▶ 4.7

▶ 4.8

Figure 4.2:
Heading

<u>IN THE COURT OF APPEAL (CIVIL DIVISION)</u>

BETWEEN:

CHARLES DICKENS

<u>Appellant</u>

-and-

HENRY CECIL

<u>Respondent</u>

SKELETON ARGUMENT
ON BEHALF OF THE APPELLANT

The heading in figure 4.2 is arranged in a distinctive way that comprises the following principal elements:

● Identity of the moot court
The name of the moot court is set out in the top left-hand corner of the heading and is underlined. For an English civil law moot, the moot court is usually the Civil Division of the Court of Appeal or the Supreme Court. For English criminal law moots, the moot court is normally

the Criminal Division of the Court of Appeal or the Supreme Court. This part of the heading therefore typically appears in one of the following three forms:

"IN THE COURT OF APPEAL (CIVIL DIVISION)"
"IN THE COURT OF APPEAL (CRIMINAL DIVISION)"
"IN THE SUPREME COURT"

● **Identity of the parties**
The full names of the parties are set out in capital letters in the middle of the page with the descriptions of each (i.e., "Appellant" and "Respondent") appearing underlined on the right-hand side of the page. When identifying natural persons in headings, include their entire names without any titles (e.g., "FRED FELIX FLINTSTONE"). Only if the moot problem does not provide an individual's first name should you use "MR", "MS", "MRS", etc. as appropriate (e.g., "MRS FLINTSTONE"). If a party is a corporate person, include in the heading the word "LIMITED" or "PLC" as the case may be (e.g., "BARNEY'S BOULDERS LIMITED").

● **Order of the parties' names**
Regardless of which side you represent, the appellant should be named in the heading before the respondent. This order reflects the fact that the first advocate to address the judge at the moot will represent the appellant. This rule applies even if, as in *Cecil v Dickens*, the claimant in the proceedings is the respondent to the appeal.

● **The word "-and-"**
In the centre of the page, between the parties' names, insert the word "-and-". Do not use the letter "v" or the word "versus". The former should be reserved for citing authorities and the latter for advertising boxing matches.

● **Identity of the party on whose behalf the skeleton argument is served**
Between "tramlines" below the names of the parties, state which party the skeleton argument is "on behalf of". Do not make the mistake of entitling your masterpiece "skeleton argument". The judge may then be forced to wade through the document to work out which side's arguments it contains.

The heading of a skeleton argument drafted on behalf of a respondent would follow exactly the same format as figure 4.2 save in one respect: the word "APPELLANT" inside the "tramlines" would be replaced by the word "RESPONDENT".

INTRODUCTION

4.9 ▶ Every skeleton argument should begin with a brief description of the case. This description should introduce the parties, explain in general terms what the case is about and state what the author is asking the court to do.

In professional practice, it is not uncommon to see skeleton arguments with introductions lasting 10 pages or more. Such prolixity is often necessary to set out the principal facts of complex cases. By contrast, introductions to moot skeleton arguments should be very short. If the competition rules impose a strict limit on the length of your skeleton, you should not waste valuable space on the introduction that is better devoted to your arguments. In any event, there is no call for long introductions in moot skeleton arguments because (unlike in professional practice) the facts are never disputed.

The facts of the moot problem can still be a source of difficulty in introductions. A common mistake is to draft an introduction that repeats, sometimes verbatim, most of the facts recited in the moot problem. Do not fall into this trap. Judges do not need to be told in your skeleton argument what the facts are; they can read the facts perfectly well in the moot problem.

Broadly speaking, there are two ways in which to draft your introduction. One is to make it very brief, literally three or four lines. The other is to produce something a little longer that incorporates some of the factual background. The choice between the two will probably be dictated by the amount of space that the competition rules allow you.

"No-frills" introduction

The short-form introduction provides a one-paragraph description of the case and requests the court to deal with it in the appropriate way—that is to say, allow the appeal (if the skeleton argument is served on behalf of the appellant) or dismiss the appeal (if it is served on the respondent's behalf). Figures 4.3 and 4.4 are examples of short-form introductions on behalf of the appellant and the respondent respectively in *Cecil v Dickens*. ▶ 4.10

Figure 4.3: ▶ 4.11
Appellant's "no-frills" introduction

[Heading]

1. This is an appeal against the decision of Steerforth J[4] upholding the claim of the Respondent ("Mr Cecil") against the Appellant ("Mr Dickens") for damages for negligent misstatement. Mr Dickens asks the court to allow the appeal on the basis that the learned judge's decision was wrong.

. . .

Figure 4.4: ▶ 4.12
Respondent's "no-frills" introduction

[Heading]

1. This is an appeal against the decision of Steerforth J upholding the claim of the Respondent ("Mr Cecil") against the Appellant ("Mr Dickens") for damages for negligent misstatement. Mr Cecil asks the court to dismiss the appeal on the basis that the learned judge's decision was correct for the reasons that he gave.

. . .

---

4   "Steerforth J" is the correct way to write the name of a High Court judge in a skeleton argument. Table 9.2 in Ch. 9 contains a comparison of the written and spoken versions of judges' titles.

Despite being drafted on behalf of opposing parties, these examples are almost identical, reflecting the limited purposes of this type of introduction. Both examples also demonstrate the use of definitions. Constant references to "the Appellant" or "the Respondent" can be confusing. Names are more likely to stick in the memory. Figures 4.3 and 4.4 therefore define the parties using their actual names: the appellant is referred to as "Mr Dickens" and the respondent as "Mr Cecil".

"With frills" introduction

4.13 ▶ The long-form introduction includes the information in the "no-frills" version, but also contains fragments of the factual background. A "with-frills" introduction should nevertheless have the same punchy quality as the short-form version. What you are aiming for is something that resembles the opening of a Lord Denning judgment.

When drafting a long-form introduction, it is important to ensure that any reference to the facts is accurate. The judge will probably read the moot problem before your skeleton and will not be impressed by an overly partisan description of the background. Of course, what you can—and, indeed, should—do is highlight in your introduction some of the facts that support your submissions.

The illustrative case of *Cecil v Dickens* can again be employed by way of example. Figure 4.5 is a possible long-form introduction to the skeleton argument of the appellant, Mr Dickens.

4.14 ▶ **Figure 4.5:**
Appellant's "with-frills" introduction

[Heading]

1. In this case, the Respondent ("Mr Cecil") alleges that the Appellant ("Mr Dickens") provided negligent advice in the course of a conversation in a pub in 2006. Mr Cecil contends that, as a result of this advice, he failed to pursue a cause of action against a firm of accountants before the relevant limitation period expired three years later.

2. At first instance, Steerforth J held that Mr Dickens owed a duty of care to Mr Cecil and breached that duty by failing to warn Mr Cecil of the existence of the limitation period. Mr Dickens appeals against both of these findings and asks the court to allow the appeal on the basis that the learned judge's decision was wrong.

. . .

Note that the example in figure 4.5 specifically mentions the given fact that the conversation between Mr Cecil and Mr Dickens took place in a pub. This fact sets the scene for Mr Dickens's argument that it would not be fair, just and reasonable to impose a duty of care for advice given in a social context. The first paragraph also makes the point that three years remained to run of the relevant limitation period when Mr Dickens advised Mr Cecil.

This fact lays the foundation for Mr Dickens's argument that it was not foreseeable that Mr Cecil would wait for such a long time before attempting to issue proceedings against the accountants.[5]

The focus of the skeleton argument on behalf of Mr Cecil would, of course, be rather different. Figure 4.6 is a possible long-form introduction to his skeleton.

Figure 4.6:
▶ 4.15
Respondent's "with-frills" introduction

[Heading]

1. In the course of a conversation during 2006, the Respondent ("Mr Cecil") asked the Appellant ("Mr Dickens"), a qualified solicitor, how to claim compensation from a firm of accountants. Although Mr Dickens told Mr Cecil that there was an arguable claim, Mr Dickens failed to mention that a limitation period applied to it. The claim became statute-barred without Mr Cecil issuing proceedings. He accordingly sued Mr Dickens for giving negligent advice.

2. At first instance, Steerforth J upheld the claim, finding that Mr Dickens owed a duty of care to Mr Cecil and that he breached that duty by failing to warn of the existence of the limitation period. Mr Dickens appeals against both of these findings. Mr Cecil asks the court to refuse the appeal on the basis that the learned judge's decision was correct for the reasons he gave.

. . .

In contrast to the example at figure 4.5, there is no mention in this introduction of the unhelpful facts that the vital conversation took place in a pub and that Mr Cecil failed to issue proceedings for three years. On the other hand, figure 4.6 does state that Mr Dickens was a qualified solicitor. This fact supports Mr Cecil's arguments that he relied on Mr Dickens's professional expertise and that the relevant standard of care was that of a solicitor rather than a non-professional.

SUBMISSIONS

The submissions are the heart of every skeleton argument. They should summarise your team's arguments on each ground of appeal. The focus of the submissions should be your team's positive case, which will already be well developed by the time you draft your skeleton. The submissions should say little, if anything, to refute the other side's case because you will not know when you draft your skeleton what the detail of your opponents' arguments will be.

▶ 4.16

---

[5] Both of the arguments referred to in this paragraph come from the possible line of argument outlined in figure 3.4 in Ch. 3.

Keys to effective submissions

4.17 ▶ Effective submissions are persuasive submissions. Persuasive submissions are logical, concise and accurate. If any one of this trinity falls by the wayside, the effectiveness of your submissions will be compromised. Each of these keys to effective submissions is therefore considered separately below.

Logic

4.18 ▶ To be persuasive, your submissions must convey the logic inherent in your arguments. As Ch. 3 explained, the form of logic that underpins most arguments at moots is deductive reasoning. Deductive reasoning involves three elements: a major premise; a minor premise; and a conclusion. When you draft skeleton arguments, you can incorporate these elements into your submissions in the following way:

A: Major premise	Identify the precise rule of law that you are advancing and refer to the authority or authorities from which you contend that the rule derives.
B: Minor premise	Explain how the rule of law on which you rely applies to the facts of the moot problem.
C: Conclusion	State the conclusion that you say results from the application of the rule of law to the facts of the moot problem.

Each argument that you make in your skeleton should include all three of these elements, even if they appear in a different order. With practice, you will find your own style of expressing and arranging arguments. It might follow the A+B=C format above. But it could equally state the conclusion up front so that the submission takes the form C=A+B. Indeed, many advocates prefer this approach because it is bold, and the judge understands from the outset where the submission is going.

You might go one step farther and use the American system for legal writing known as "CRAC". CRAC stands for "Conclusion. Rule. Analysis. Conclusion." Under this system, the "Rule" section of a written argument is the major premise in deductive reasoning and the "Analysis" section is the minor premise. The only difference between CRAC and the C=A+B approach is that, with CRAC, the conclusion is set out at both the beginning and the end of the argument.

What you must not do when drafting submissions is make the mistake of simply rephrasing the grounds of appeal. A submission of this sort on behalf of the appellant, Mr Dickens, might look like this:

> *"For Mr Dickens to be liable to Mr Cecil, Mr Dickens must have owed a duty of care to Mr Cecil when they met in January 2006. The requirements for a duty of care to arise were not met. No duty of care therefore arose."*

This submission contains no statement of the rule governing when duties of care in negligence arise (the major premise) nor any explanation of how that rule applies to the facts of *Cecil v Dickens* (the minor premise). The submission consequently lacks any logical reasoning and will not persuade the judge.

Your submissions must not only convey the logic inherent in your argument, they must also be arranged in a logical order. Whilst common sense should point you in the right direction most of the time, make sure that you adhere to these two guidelines:

● **Address the grounds of appeal in the order they appear in the moot problem**
There are usually at least two grounds of appeal in a moot problem and they are set out in a particular order. Unless you have a very good reason for departing from this order, stick to it when you arrange the submissions in your skeleton argument. The author of the moot problem, usually a lecturer in law or a practitioner, will have given some thought to the order in which the grounds of appeal are arranged. There will therefore be logic behind it. The problem in the illustrative case of *Cecil v Dickens*, for example, identifies two grounds of appeal: the first is concerned with the existence of a duty of care; the second with whether any duty was breached. This is the logical order for your submissions because the issue of breach of duty arises only if a duty exists in the first place.

● **For each ground of appeal, lead with your strongest point**
In relation to any particular ground of appeal, you may have two or more submissions to make. One of those submissions will usually be stronger than the other(s). Lead with that point. In this way, your submissions should have the greatest impact on the judge. If the leading point is strong, the judge will be more inclined to regard your subsequent (and weaker) arguments as bolstering it. Conversely, starting off with a poor point may "infect" those that follow and make you less credible generally.

Conciseness   ▷ **4.19**
Skeleton arguments should be short; they are not called *skeleton* arguments for nothing. Your submissions should therefore be limited to the bare "bones" of your arguments. You may, of course, have no option but to write short submissions if your skeleton is subject to a stringent page or word limit. But there are at least two good reasons for keeping your submissions concise even if you are free from such a restriction.

First, you need to hold something back for the moot. If you spell out every aspect of each argument in your skeleton, you will leave yourself with nothing new to say during your oral submissions. You then face the danger that your speech becomes a mere canter through your skeleton argument. No judge will be impressed by that approach.

The second reason for keeping your submissions succinct is to minimise your opponents' understanding of your case. You will have to exchange your skeleton argument with the other side in advance of the moot. Whilst formidable opponents will anticipate much of your positive case even before seeing your skeleton, there is no need to spoon-feed them the nitty-gritty. Let them spend some of their precious preparation time thinking about how the detail might flow from your written submissions, and force them to listen carefully to what you say at the moot.

Conciseness refers not only to the length of the submissions in your skeleton argument, but also to the language that you use. Persuasive language is usually short and pithy. Convoluted language, by contrast, suggests that the point being made is weak or that the draftsman has not thought it through properly. Or both.

Accuracy

4.20 ▶ Lawyers are perfectionists and their stock-in-trade is accuracy of expression. Your written submissions must be accurate too. Whenever you refer to an authority, for example, the citation must be correct. Make a mistake and you may lose credibility with the judge if the error comes to light at the moot. Ensuring that your citations of authority are accurate is all about attention to detail. You should therefore check and double-check them all. Do not rely on citations of law reports contained in textbooks and articles. They are wrong more often than you might think. Instead, always check the primary source—the report itself.

It is not just your citations of authority that must be accurate. Any reference that you make in your submissions—for example to the facts of the moot problem—must be correct. Your submissions must also be *written* accurately. They must be spelled correctly, properly punctuated and free from grammatical errors. Correct English usage is relevant to the whole of your skeleton argument, not just the submissions, and it is accordingly considered in more detail later in this chapter.

Referring to authorities

4.21 ▶ As the beginning of this chapter explained, your submissions should refer to each of the authorities on which your team will rely at the moot. In order to assist the judge and your opponents, every reference to authority in your submissions should be as precise as possible, preferably identifying the page or paragraph number of each relevant passage.

The following guidance on drafting references to authority focuses on three issues: the format of citations; citing cases that appear in multiple series of law reports; and quoting from authorities.

Format of citations

4.22 ▶ There is no universally applied format for the citation of authorities in England and Wales. Some advocates underline the names of parties in case citations, for example, while others use italics. It is nonetheless a good idea to follow in your skeleton arguments the format for citation employed by the *Law Reports*, the most authoritative series of English case reports. The essential features of this format for different types of authority are set out below:

● **Reported cases**

The names of the parties and the letter "v" that divides them are in italics. The remainder of the citation is not italicised. When reference is made to a particular page of a judgment, the page number is added at the end of the citation together (if appropriate) with the name of the judge. The result is a citation that looks like this:

Donoghue v Stevenson [1932] AC 562, 580 per Lord Atkin

● **Unreported cases**

The names of the parties appear as in reported cases, but they are followed by the word "unreported" in parentheses and the date on which the judgment was handed down. The date is written long-hand. The citation thus appears as follows:

Martine v South East Kent Health Authority (unreported), 25 February 1993

● **Textbooks**

The author's name (in italics) is followed by the title (also in italics), the edition, the year of publication (in parentheses) and the volume number (if appropriate). A page reference can be added thereafter. The following examples are textbook citations (as it were):

Clerk & Lindsell on Torts, 20th ed (2013), p.460

David Pope and Dan Hill, Mooting and Advocacy Skills, 3rd ed (2015), p.15

● **Journal articles**

The full name of the author is followed by the title of the article, which is placed in quotation marks. The journal citation comes next. None of the citation is italicised. The following is an example:

Jane Stapleton, "Duty of Care and Economic Loss: A Wider Agenda" (1991) 107 LQR 249

Whatever format you employ when citing authorities, you must be consistent throughout your skeleton argument. Do not use one format for your first citation and a different format for the next.

Citing cases reported in multiple series

Cases are regularly reported in more than one series of law reports. For example, the Court of Appeal's decision in *Chaudhry v Prabhakar*, which is relevant to the illustrative moot problem of *Cecil v Dickens*, is reported both at [1989] 1 WLR 29 and [1988] 3 All ER 718. When faced with this situation, which citation should you use in your skeleton argument? Ideally, you should cite the report in the series that appears highest in the hierarchy of law reports set out in figure 4.7. You would therefore cite the version of *Chaudhry v Prabhakar* that appears in the *Weekly Law Reports*.

⟩ 4.23

The hierarchy in figure 4.7 is not universally observed, even among practising lawyers. You are therefore unlikely to be penalised for using one of the lesser series of reports when a more authoritative alternative exists. However, the *Law Reports* and the *Weekly Law Reports* do have three distinct advantages over the other series. First, every judgment is approved for publication by the judge who gave it. There is accordingly a decreased risk of a mistake appearing in the text. Second, both the *Law Reports* and the *Weekly Law Reports* include summaries of the arguments of counsel. As discussed in Ch. 3, these summaries can be a fertile source of inspiration for arguments. Finally, the *Law Reports* in particular often include the judgments of both the lower and appeal courts in the same report.[6] You may consequently be saved the trouble of checking whether a particular decision was appealed. These factors provide a major incentive for using the *Law Reports* or the *Weekly Law Reports* whenever possible.

Quoting from authorities

During your legal research, you may find an especially helpful passage in a particular authority that neatly encapsulates a point that you wish to make at the moot. It could be a statement of legal principle in a case report or a pithy summary of the law in a practitioner

⟩ 4.24

---

[6] It was the absence of this feature that led the Court of Appeal to criticise the citation of the *All England Law Reports* in *Governor and Company of the Bank of Scotland v Henry Butcher & Co.* [2003] 2 All ER (Comm) 557.

4.25 ▷

Figure 4.7:
Hierarchy of English law reports

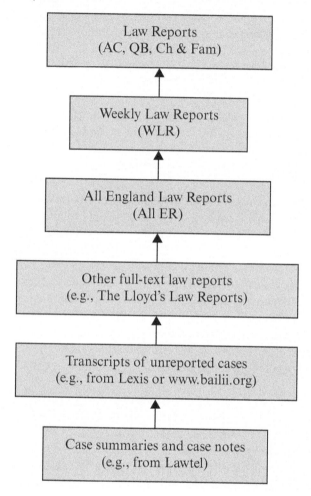

textbook. Space permitting, there is nothing to stop you from quoting the passage in your skeleton argument. If you take this course, however, the watchword is "brevity". The imported text should be short—no more than about five lines. Remember that you can always take the judge through a longer extract of the authority during your oral submissions at the moot.

If the moot problem turns on the construction of a particular statutory provision, it is usually a good idea to quote it in full in your skeleton argument. That advice holds good even if the provision is set out in the moot problem because the judge will still benefit from having the relevant wording in the same document as your submissions. Use common sense, however. If the statutory provision runs to more than five lines or so, it is likely to be too long to replicate in full. You should then consider quoting only the most important phrases.

CONCLUSION

Last, and in this instance least, comes the conclusion of the skeleton argument. In fact, it is perfectly acceptable to dispense with a conclusion altogether and end your skeleton with the last of your substantive submissions. Nonetheless, if you have some space at the end of your skeleton, it is worth rounding it off with a short sentence stating what it is that you want the court to do. There is no harm, after all, in applying the old adage, "Tell 'em what you're going to tell 'em (introduction); then tell 'em (submissions); then tell 'em what you told 'em (conclusion)".

▶ 4.26

If you represent the appellant, your final paragraph will request the court to allow the appeal. If you act for the respondent, it will ask the court to dismiss the appeal. The following sentence, amended as appropriate, will cover either eventuality: "It is accordingly submitted that the appeal should be allowed/dismissed."

If you have space to spare, you can draft a slightly more elaborate conclusion that reiterates the particular finding or findings that you would like the court to make. Figure 4.8 shows a possible concluding paragraph in the skeleton argument of the appellant in *Cecil v Dickens*.

Figure 4.8:
Conclusion

▶ 4.27

. . .

7.   For the reasons set out above, it is submitted that the court should allow the appeal and find that Mr Dickens owed no duty of care to Mr Cecil or, alternatively, that Mr Dickens did not breach any duty that he did owe to Mr Cecil.

. . .

After the text of the conclusion, at the right-hand side of the final page of your skeleton argument, set out on separate lines the names of the members of your team in the order in which they will address the moot court. Below the names of the mooters, but on the left-hand side of the page, insert the date on which you will serve your skeleton argument.

Figure 4.9 shows how the names and dates would appear on a skeleton argument served by a mooting team comprising CJ Stryver as leading counsel and Sydney Carton as junior counsel.

Figure 4.9:
Names and date

▶ 4.28

7. [Final paragraph]

CJ Stryver

Sydney Carton

19 January 2015

THE FINISHED ARTICLE

4.29 ▶ You now have the building blocks with which to construct a skeleton argument. So that you can see what the final edifice looks like, figure 4.10 is an example of a complete skeleton on behalf of the appellant in *Cecil v Dickens*. It draws together figures 4.2 (heading), 4.3 (appellant's "no-frills" introduction), 4.8 (conclusion) and 4.9 (names and date), and includes possible submissions on both grounds of appeal. The submissions on the first ground of appeal are based on the line of argument summarised in figure 3.4 in Ch. 3. Figure 4.10 assumes that the competition rules allow each team to cite just three authorities.

4.30 ▶ **Figure 4.10:**
Complete skeleton argument

IN THE COURT OF APPEAL (CIVIL DIVISION)

BETWEEN:

CHARLES DICKENS

Appellant

-and-

HENRY CECIL

Respondent

SKELETON ARGUMENT
ON BEHALF OF THE APPELLANT

1. This is an appeal against the decision of Steerforth J upholding the claim of the Respondent ("Mr Cecil") against the Appellant ("Mr Dickens") for damages for negligent misstatement. Mr Dickens asks the court to allow the appeal on the basis that the learned judge's decision was wrong.

First Ground of Appeal: Duty of Care

2. The modern approach to imposing duties of care in negligence to avoid pure economic loss is set out in *Customs and Excise Commissioners v Barclays Bank plc* [2007] 1 AC 181. None of the tests that the House of Lords applied in that case is satisfied here. In particular:

   (1) There was no assumption of responsibility because Mr Dickens expressly told Mr Cecil to consult solicitors who specialised in litigation.

(2) It was not reasonably foreseeable that Mr Cecil would delay for more than three years before consulting litigation solicitors.

(3) It would not be fair, just and reasonable to impose a duty of care given that Mr Dickens provided advice to a friend in a social setting.

3. In addition, as a matter of policy, the imposition of a duty of care in this case would considerably extend liability in negligence for pure economic loss.

4. It is accordingly submitted that Mr Dickens owed no duty of care to Mr Cecil.

Second Ground of Appeal: Breach of Duty

5. If, contrary to his primary case, Mr Dickens owed a duty of care to Mr Cecil, the relevant standard of care is that of a reasonably competent solicitor: *Green v Collyer-Bristow* [1999] Lloyd's Rep. PN 798. Further, Mr Dickens's duty was not to take every possible care: *Winfield & Jolowicz, Tort*, 19th ed (2014), para. 12-035.

6. Mr Dickens satisfied the relevant standard when he told Mr Cecil to consult specialist litigation solicitors if he decided to pursue a claim against Wickfield's. It is accordingly submitted that Mr Dickens did not breach any duty that he owed to Mr Cecil.

Conclusion

7. For the reasons set out above, it is submitted that the court should allow the appeal and find that Mr Dickens owed no duty of care to Mr Cecil or, alternatively, that Mr Dickens did not breach any duty that he did owe to Mr Cecil.

CJ Stryver

Sydney Carton

19 January 2015

SPELLING, GRAMMAR AND PUNCTUATION

Moot skeleton arguments may be short pieces of prose, but they must still exhibit all of the key features of good legal writing. First among those features is proper English usage: an absence of spelling errors and conformity to the rules of English grammar and punctuation. This section explains why correct English usage matters in skeleton arguments, identifies some of the most common errors that mooters make and provides advice on how to avoid mistakes.   ▶ 4.31

Importance of correct English usage

It has been fashionable for some time to downplay the significance of correct English usage. Whatever the merits of that view in other walks of life, it holds little sway in the law. Lawyers   ▶ 4.32

are paid large sums of money to convey ideas and information accurately. Get it wrong, particularly in writing, and the consequences can be disastrous. The law reports are full of disputes about the meanings of words and phrases. Several cases—and perhaps a few livelihoods—have been lost over the position of a comma.

Proper English usage is especially important in skeleton arguments. Errors of spelling, grammar and punctuation in skeletons have two particular effects that can seriously undermine the persuasiveness of your arguments: loss of credibility and loss of comprehension.

Loss of credibility

4.33 ▶ Mistakes in English usage send a clear message: either you do not know how to write English correctly or you are too lazy to bother. In either event, this message will damage your credibility with the judge. As Aristotle explained, credibility—or ēthos—is possibly the most important factor in persuasion. Advocates without credibility rarely persuade judges. Blow your credibility and you could blow the moot.

To make matters worse, sloppy English has a particularly marked impact on credibility when it appears in skeleton arguments. A skeleton usually provides the judge with his or her first impression of any mooter. As numerous psychological studies have shown, first impressions are hard to shift. You may therefore struggle to displace the negative impression created by a skeleton argument littered with spelling errors, even with an accomplished performance at the moot.

Loss of comprehension

4.34 ▶ Spelling, grammatical and punctuation mistakes create uncertainties in meaning. Sometimes a mistake is such that the reader can nevertheless discern what the author meant. "No harm done", you might think. But a moot judge may still resent having to root around for a meaning that ought to have been explicit.

The damage will be infinitely greater if the mistake generates ambiguity or incomprehensibility. The judge will then not only resent having to make unsuccessful efforts to divine a clear meaning from your prose, but he or she will also not understand your point. Needless to say, a judge who does not follow an argument will not be persuaded by it.

Common mistakes

4.35 ▶ Some errors of spelling, grammar and punctuation are more common than others. Whole books and innumerable websites are devoted to them. A small sub-set of those mistakes crops up time and again in moot skeleton arguments. Nine of these repeat offenders are described below. Make sure you avoid them.

Common spelling mistakes

4.36 ▶ ● **"Its" and "it's"**
The possessive pronoun "its" is often misspelled "it's", apparently in the erroneous belief that an apostrophe is needed to indicate ownership. Several other possessive pronouns, particularly "hers", "yours" and "theirs", cause similar confusion. None of them takes an apostrophe. An asset owned by a company is therefore "its asset" and your car is "yours".

The word "it's", by contrast, is a contraction of "it is", just as the word "isn't" is a contraction of the word "is not". Contractions are informal and, as such, should not appear in skeleton arguments.

● "Judgement" and "judgment"
Moot skeleton arguments frequently refer to court decisions as "judgements". In legal writing, however, this type of "judgment" has one "e", not two. The main meaning of "judgement" with a second "e" is "the ability to make considered decisions or come to sensible conclusions"[7] (as in "he lacks judgement").

● "Practice" and "practise"
The words "practice" (with a second "c") and "practise" (with an "s") are often used interchangeably. But in British English (as opposed to American English), the former is a noun and the latter a verb.[8] So, a successful solicitor might "own a legal practice" (noun) and "practise law" (verb).

● "Principal" and "principle"
These two words have very different meanings, yet they are regularly used in place of one another. The word "principal" (ending "pal") is most commonly used as an adjective to mean "main" or "most important".[9] A mooter might therefore correctly refer to her "principal submission". The word "principle" (ending "ple") is normally used as a noun meaning "a fundamental basis of a system of thought or belief".[10] It appears most frequently in the expression "in principle", which means "as a general idea or plan".[11]

Common grammatical mistakes
● Subject and verb disagreements

▷ 4.37

A verb must agree with its subject in number (i.e., singular or plural). A singular subject must therefore have a singular verb and a plural subject must have a plural verb. Mooters often make agreement errors when they use certain words. For example, the words "criteria", "data" and "media" are commonly given singular verbs even though they are all plural. Conversely, the indefinite pronouns "each" and "either" require singular verb forms. It is therefore incorrect to write that, "Either of these arguments determine the case". The correct version of this sentence is, "Either of these arguments *determines* the case".

● Pronoun and antecedent disagreements
A pronoun and the word to which it refers (the antecedent) must also agree in number. When the subject of a sentence is singular, for example, a pronoun that stands in for it later in the text must also be singular. The most common mistake that mooters make in this regard is to use the plural pronoun "their" when they ought to use a singular pronoun (typically

---

[7] *The New Oxford Dictionary of English*, 1998.
[8] In American English, both the noun and the verb are spelled with a second "c".
[9] *The New Oxford Dictionary of English*, 1998.
[10] *The New Oxford Dictionary of English*, 1998.
[11] *The New Oxford Dictionary of English*, 1998.

"his", "her" or "its"). A skeleton might, for instance, say that, 'The appellant submits that the court should accept their primary submission". Since the word "appellant" in this sentence is a singular noun, the pronoun "their" should be replaced with "his", "her" or "its" as the case may be.

Common punctuation mistakes

4.38 ▷ ● **Redundant semicolons**

Semicolons sometimes appear in moot skeleton arguments for no apparent reason, suggesting that the authors were unclear how to use this punctuation mark. It is appropriate in two main circumstances. The first is to join two related independent clauses (i.e., clauses that could stand on their own as full sentences). For example, a skeleton might properly end with these words: "The appellant requests the court to allow the appeal; the learned judge's decision was plainly wrong." The second principal use of semicolons is to separate items in a series. Commas are normally used for this purpose, but they can lead to confusion, particularly if elements of the series are themselves lists. Semicolons help to clarify the meaning of the following sentence, for example: "Liability is imposed in negligence if it is fair, just and reasonable for a duty of care to arise; the duty is breached; and the requirements of causation, remoteness and damage are satisfied."

● **Comma splices with the word "however"**

A comma splice is the incorrect use of a comma to join into one sentence what should be two sentences or independent clauses. Comma splices occur most frequently in moot skeleton arguments when students use the word "however" in the mistaken belief that it is a coordinating conjunction like "and" or "but". The following sentence is a typical example of this type of comma splice: "The factual position is straightforward, however, the legal position is complex." The error in this sentence could be corrected in one of two ways. The first is to replace the comma before the word "however" with a semicolon. The sentence would then read, "The factual position is straightforward; however, the legal position is complex." Alternatively, the sentence could be broken into two as follows: "The factual position is straightforward. However, the legal position is complex."

● **Apostrophes to form plurals**

Apostrophes are not needed to make nouns plural. This rule is most commonly breached in the context of plurals of numbers. A moot skeleton argument might, for example, refer to the "1990's" or a person in her "80's". Neither apostrophe is correct. It was the "1990s", and an octogenarian is in her "80s".

How to avoid mistakes

4.39 ▷ Although spelling errors are the most common form of mistaken English usage, they are also the easiest to eradicate. There is some truth in the adage that a good speller is a good dictionary-user. If you are in any doubt about the spelling of a particular word—any doubt at all—look it up in a dictionary. Do not rely on computer spell-checkers as they often fail to spot mistakes.

Assistance is also on hand to remedy mistakes of grammar and punctuation. Informative websites abound. A good example is *http://owl.english.purdue.edu*, which is the online writing lab of Purdue University in the United States. In addition, a veritable library of books exists on English usage. The granddaddy of them all is *Fowler's Modern English Usage*, Re-revised 3rd ed, 2004. Generations of writers, journalists and lawyers (among others) have sworn by it. *Fowler's* is not the most user-friendly book, however. By contrast, *The Hodges Harbrace Handbook*, 18th ed, 2012 is practical and easy to use. It is written by Americans for Americans, but Brits and others can readily use it too. And if you want to have a good laugh while learning the rules of grammar and punctuation, read *Lynne Truss, Eats, Shoots and Leaves*, 2009 (paperback edition).

LEGAL WRITING CONVENTIONS

Lawyers observe certain conventions when they write formal prose. A breach of one of these conventions is not a mistake of usage, but it is a mistake nevertheless. It will reveal you as a novice as yet untutored in the ways of the legal community.

▶ 4.40

Four of the most important legal writing conventions are described below:

● **Never write in the first person**

As a mooter, you advance arguments on behalf of fictitious "clients". Your role is akin to that of a hired gun. Do not therefore express your submissions in the first person as if they were your own views. It is the judge's prerogative to express personal opinions, not yours. You should consequently avoid phrases such as, "In my/our opinion, ...", "It seems to me/us that ..." and "I/We think that ..." In their stead, use expressions such as, "In my/our submission, ...", "It is submitted that ..." and "The appellant/respondent submits that ..."

● **Avoid colloquialisms, slang and contractions**

Do not use colloquialisms (words or phrases characteristic of informal speech), slang or contractions of words or phrases. Skeleton arguments should have a professional tone. The tone of your skeleton will be lowered if you use informal language. A skeleton argument for *Cecil v Dickens* should not therefore state that, "The parties were two *pals* who went for a *pint* at their *local*", but rather, "The parties were long-standing friends who met for a drink at a local pub."

● **Avoid excessively formal language**

Conversely, modern legal writing may be formal, but not to the point of pomposity or obfuscation. Thanks in part to the "Plain English" movement, lawyers have largely come to realise that their writing should be comprehensible to laymen. Skeleton arguments should therefore be free from Latin, unless there really is no sensible English alternative,[12] and devoid of stuffy lawyerisms like "heretofore", "aforementioned" and "said" used as an adjective (as in "the said meeting").

---

12 An example of a Latin expression that has become a term of art, and is therefore acceptable, is *"res ipsa loquitur"*.

● **Steer clear of inflammatory language**

Few judges, whether sitting in a moot court or any other court, are impressed by the use of extravagant adjectives such as "outrageous", "appalling" and "hopeless".[13] Even if your opponent's submissions really are "outrageous" and "hopeless", you can be confident that the judge will know without help from you. Inflammatory language may not only irritate the judge, but also cause confusion. A case in point is the word "gross". Do not place it before the word "negligence", however tempting it may be to emphasise a defendant's wrongdoing. The expression "gross negligence" has a long and unhappy history. If you use it, you may find yourself having to explain the precise difference between "gross negligence" and "ordinary negligence".

FORMAT

4.41 ▶ Tempting though it may be to believe that the judge will be interested only in the forcefulness of the submissions contained in your skeleton argument, the truth is that he or she will also be influenced to some extent by the way in which those submissions are packaged. In other words, presentation matters.

Thankfully, it is not that difficult to get the format of skeleton arguments right. Indeed, the surprising thing is that so many advocates, even those in professional practice, get it so wrong.[14] What follows is a brief checklist of the "rules" of presentation.

● **Type it up**

In these days of omnipresent PCs, this advice may be unnecessary, but never be tempted to write out your skeleton argument long-hand. However neat your handwriting may be, a typed document will always be easier on the eye and look more professional than a manuscript document.

● **Print on one side of the page only**

Unless the competition rules say otherwise, keep the text of your skeleton argument to one side of each sheet of paper and leave the other side blank. Double-sided documents are less easy to read.

● **Use paragraph numbers**

Every paragraph of your skeleton argument should be numbered consecutively. The judge can then find particular passages quickly and without fuss when you refer to them at the moot.

● **Insert page numbers**

For the same reason, any skeleton argument that exceeds one page should be consecutively numbered at the bottom of each page.

---

[13] In *Sony Computer Entertainment Europe Limited v Commissioners for Her Majesty's Revenue and Customs* [2006] EWCA Civ 772; [2006] All ER (D) 164, for example, the Court of Appeal castigated a skeleton argument for its "*frequent and unnecessary resort to hyperbole*".

[14] For a judge's take on the repeated failures of the barristers appearing before him to produce skeleton arguments in an appropriate format, see Mr Justice James Hunt, "The Anatomy Lesson", Counsel, February 2002.

● **Allow generous spacing and margins**

If possible, your skeleton argument should be double-spaced and have decent margins on either side of the page. The judge (whose eyesight may not be what it once was) will find your skeleton easier to read and will have some space in which to jot down notes.

● **Use headings**

Even relatively short skeleton arguments benefit from two or three headings. For more lengthy skeletons, headings are essential if the judge is to make quick sense of the arguments that you are advancing. There is no need to go overboard, however. Headings are useful for distinguishing between the principal parts of your skeleton, such as the submissions on each ground of appeal, but their utility is lost if every paragraph has one.

● **Avoid footnotes**

Multiple footnotes may impress the editors of law reviews, but they will not endear you to moot tribunals. The judge wants to understand from your skeleton argument what your case is without having to refer constantly to screeds of microscopic writing at the bottom of each page. Although footnotes can very occasionally assist a skeleton argument, they are generally best avoided.

● **Avoid small or idiosyncratic fonts**

If possible, stick to 11- or 12-pitch text size and Times New Roman or Arial font when drafting your skeleton arguments. Judges should not have to pull out magnifying glasses to read your submissions. They may also question your sanity if you use an overly elaborate font. *This sort of thing, for example.*

DEALING WITH MISTAKES

It is possible to make all sorts of mistakes when drafting skeleton arguments. This section examines two types: errors of drafting and missing the deadline for exchange. ▶ **4.42**

Mistakes of drafting

However many times you read your skeleton argument before exchange, it may still harbour a drafting error of some description. How you deal with that mistake if you discover it before the moot will depend on its seriousness and, potentially, the competition rules. ▶ **4.43**

Three types of mistake that it is possible to make in a skeleton argument are described below in ascending order of magnitude together with the approaches that you might sensibly consider taking to deal with them. None of these suggestions should be taken as gospel. You must apply common sense to the circumstances that confront you.

Errors of spelling, grammar and punctuation

Unfortunate though they are, the best policy is almost always to live with mistakes of this nature. However, if in the course of your oral submissions, you need to refer the judge to a passage of your skeleton argument that includes an error of English usage that in some way obscures the point you are trying to make, you can always correct it "on the hoof". ▶ **4.44**

Incorrect citations

4.45 ▶ Mistakes of this type cannot be so easily ignored. If your skeleton argument refers to the wrong page or volume number of a law report, for example, the incorrect citation could cause confusion to the judge and your opponents. In those circumstances, you should attempt to rectify the error as quickly as possible by notifying the judge and the other side of the correct citation. If they are not readily contactable, you may have to ask the moot organiser to let them know.

Unarguable submissions

4.46 ▶ It is possible that, after exchange, you realise that one of the submissions in your skeleton argument is not properly arguable. Your opponents' skeleton might, for example, refer to a binding authority of which you were previously unaware that conclusively rebuts a written submission that you have made. Be wary of reaching this conclusion too quickly. There is often a "heart in the mouth" moment when you see your opponents' skeleton for the first time. Inevitably, they will not have approached things in the same way as you and you may initially feel that their approach is more convincing. But that is very different from discovering that one of your submissions is wholly without foundation.

If that unfortunate eventuality does arise (and it should be a very rare event), your best course is to deal with the point in oral submissions at the moot. If you can concoct an alternative way of arguing the point that does not suffer from the same fatal flaw, so much the better. If not, you can simply inform the judge that you are no longer pursuing the submission. You may even be able to turn the misfortune to your advantage if you can demonstrate to the judge your ability to accept the force of the other side's point, but then move the argument swiftly onto more solid ground.

Missing the deadline for exchange

4.47 ▶ In professional practice, advocates who serve their skeleton arguments late are required to explain in a personal letter to the judge why they missed the deadline. The consequences of late exchange in a moot can be similarly unwelcome. At the very least, the judge is likely to take late service of your skeleton into account in determining who wins the moot. In a close contest, compliance with the competition rules can be the deciding factor.

Worse still is the possibility that, if the delay is significant, you may be forced to concede the moot altogether. The moot organiser will not take that step lightly. But however slim the chances might be, you do not want to take the risk. Get your skeleton in on time.

CHAPTER CHECKLIST

4.48 ▶
- Give your skeleton argument the proper heading.
- Start your skeleton argument with a short introduction that identifies the parties, explains what the case is about and states what you are asking the court to do.
- Draft submissions that are logical, concise and accurate.
- If space permits, end your skeleton argument with a short conclusion.

- Punctuate your skeleton argument properly and avoid spelling and grammatical errors.
- Observe the conventions of legal writing.
- Present your skeleton argument in an attractive and readable format.
- Use common sense to deal with any mistakes in your skeleton argument.

▶ 5
Speaking notes

5.1 ▶ Most mooters enter the moot courtroom clutching a sheaf of notes to assist them with their speeches. Yet, all too often, those notes prove to be more of a hindrance than a help. Many perfectly able mooters shackle themselves unnecessarily to full written speeches that they then proceed to read. Others take the opposite path, relying on minimal notes that leave them floundering for words at critical moments in their oral submissions.

This chapter explores the skills required to draft effective notes for moot speeches. It begins by exposing some of the myths surrounding speaking notes and identifies the principal functions that notes should perform. It then analyses various styles of notes—full written speeches, outlines and ad hoc forms—before offering several tips for note-drafting that apply whichever style you adopt. The chapter concludes by describing the different media on which speaking notes can be written.

SOME MYTHS ABOUT SPEAKING NOTES

5.2 ▶ Few aspects of mooting have generated as much hokum as the speaking notes that mooters should use. Even a cursory surf on the internet uncovered the following dubious pronouncements on the subject:

- *"It is advisable . . . always to use cards rather than paper."*
- *"Barristers in practice . . . rarely speak from more than the skeleton argument that they have exchanged with the other side."*
- *"In no circumstances should you have a 'speech' written out in full."*

None of these statements is true. While using cards works for some mooters, most prefer other media for their notes. Practising barristers almost always use notes in addition to their skeleton arguments. And while relying on a full written speech undoubtedly carries risks, it is certainly not a bar to effective advocacy.

In truth, drafting speaking notes is a matter of personal preference. The critical consideration is whether your notes work for you. Do they, in other words, fulfil all of the functions that effective speaking notes must perform?

FUNCTIONS OF SPEAKING NOTES

Whether your speaking notes are brief or bloated, typed up or scribbled in manuscript, they should play three main roles: a prompt; a flexible reference; and a comfort blanket. Although there is a significant overlap between them, each of these roles is discussed separately below.

▶ 5.3

A prompt

Mooters make speeches lasting 10 minutes or more about complex areas of the law. Even with thorough preparation, few people can deliver such a speech entirely from memory.

▶ 5.4

The first task of your notes is therefore to provide you with a prompt. As you are speaking, you should be able to look down at your notes, find the right place in them and be reminded of the information that you need in order to make your next point to the judge. If your notes are an effective prompt, you will be able to do all of this quickly and with minimal interruption to your train of speech. Conversely, signs that your notes are not providing a sufficient prompt include running out of things to say, punctuating your oral submissions with frequent "ums" and "errs", losing the thread of your argument and failing to maintain eye contact with the judge.

A flexible reference

One of the most challenging aspects of mooting is adapting your oral submissions as events unfold at the moot. You are most likely to be blown off course by questions from the judge. They may force you to recast a submission that you were going to make or to re-order some of your points. You might also have to spend more time on a particular topic than you had originally intended, perhaps because the judge has shown particular interest in it or your opponents have unexpectedly "majored" in it.

▶ 5.5

The second main function of your speaking notes is therefore to provide a flexible reference. Notes with the requisite degree of flexibility will allow you to jump around from one topic to another without losing your place. They will also enable you to compress or expand your submissions as the clock requires.

A comfort blanket

Mooting is a stressful business. It requires a high degree of concentration, involves the marshalling of numerous facts and documents, and takes place in public.

▶ 5.6

The third task of your speaking notes is therefore to provide you with a modicum of comfort, a safe haven to which you can retreat if your memory fails you or your composure is momentarily rattled. Plenty of mooters have little need of a comfort blanket, being naturally self-assured. But most do like to have something to fall back on.

STYLES OF SPEAKING NOTES

Although there are doubtless mooters out there who have perfected the art of making sensational oral submissions from nothing more than a flow chart, most ordinary mortals' speaking notes fall into one of three categories: a full written speech; an outline; or an ad hoc form of

▶ 5.7

notes. Each of these styles is examined below. None should be regarded as the paradigm. Different styles of notes work equally effectively for different people. What counts is not so much the form that your notes take as the way in which you use them.

Written speeches

What is a written speech?

5.8 ▷ A written speech is a longhand version of the words that you intend to utter at the moot. It is, in effect, a script for your oral submissions. Figure 5.1 shows what the start of the speaking notes of the first mooter for the appellant in *Cecil v Dickens* might look like if written out in full.[1]

5.9 ▷ **Figure 5.1:**
Example written speech

My Lord, I appear on behalf of the appellant in this matter, Mr Charles Dickens, together with my learned friend Sydney Carton. The respondent, Mr Henry Cecil, is represented by my learned friends Sally Mannering and Roger Thursby.

This is the hearing of the appeal against the decision of Mr Justice Steerforth, sitting in the Queen's Bench Division, that Mr Dickens gave negligent advice to Mr Cecil in relation to a potential claim by Mr Cecil against a firm of accountants called Wickfield's.

Mr Dickens appeals against the decision of the learned judge on two grounds. The first is that Mr Dickens owed no duty of care to Mr Cecil. I intend to address Your Lordship on this ground of appeal. The second is that, even if a duty of care was owed to Mr Cecil, Mr Dickens did not breach it. My learned friend Mr Carton will address Your Lordship on that ground of appeal.

. . .

Advantages and disadvantages of written speeches

5.10 ▷ Written speeches certainly provide the greatest level of comfort to mooters. If you are stricken with nerves or your memory freezes, you can revert to your speech and read it to the end. It may not be pretty and it may not win you the moot, but you will at least make it through your oral submissions. It is no doubt for this, entirely understandable, reason that most novice mooters tend towards this approach when drafting their speaking notes.

However, whilst a written speech is the ultimate comfort blanket, it is considerably less effective as a prompt. Indeed, rather than prompting submissions, written speeches tend to lead mooters to read verbatim. If you read, your head will be almost constantly down, you will not project your voice effectively, you will avoid eye contact with the judge and your delivery will be stilted and unnatural (it being very difficult to write prose in precisely the way you speak). In short, you will find it hard to engage the judge with what you are saying, however compelling the substance of your submissions might be.

Written speeches are also inflexible. Being overly reliant on a written speech makes it

---

[1] Ch. 10 examines each element of these opening remarks in detail.

hard to compress or expand your oral submissions as the circumstances of the moot demand. Equally, written speeches do not serve mooters well when judges ask questions. Typically, mooters are thrown off course either because they cannot find the passage in their speech that deals with the judge's point or because, having answered the question, they cannot re-find the correct place in their speech from which to resume their submissions. Many is the mooter in this latter situation who has mistakenly returned to the wrong spot in his or her script and re-read a paragraph or two without realising it.

What is more, many moot judges are extremely intolerant of students who read speeches. If one of those judges sees you reading—and it is usually easy to tell—he or she will probably mark you down.

Drafting a full written speech therefore has its pitfalls. Many of them can be avoided, however, if you take suitable precautions. The key, remember, is not to *read* your speech at the moot. You will therefore have to memorise sections of your speech to the point where you can recite them naturally. You will also have to know the material intimately so that you can deal fluently with questions from the judge. In addition, you will need to develop a system for maintaining the right place in your speaking notes when the judge intervenes. It might be as simple as keeping your finger pressed to the spot that you had reached in your script. Alternatively, you might mark that point with a pen or highlighter.

If you can manage the drawbacks effectively, it is perfectly possible to make persuasive—and winning—submissions using this style of speaking notes. Indeed, there are plenty of successful QCs who write out in advance virtually every word they utter in court. And do not take our word for it. John Kelsey-Fry QC, one of the luminaries of the English libel bar, which is hardly a bastion for the faint-hearted, described his method of preparing for hearings in this way:

> *"I type up every single word of my speeches including the apparent ad libs and asides. . . . I avoid lawyers' words at all costs and will rewrite a speech ten times until it fits."[2]*

Outlines
What is an outline?
At the other end of the note-drafting spectrum from the written speech is the outline. An outline conveys the logic and structure of your argument, typically without resorting to complete sentences. It generally consists of a series of assertions and references placed on the page in several levels of indentation. Its success as a form of notes largely depends on the mooter's ability to strike the right balance between excessive detail and insufficient information. Figure 5.2 is an example of an outline that covers the opening remarks that appeared as a full written speech in figure 5.1.

▶ 5.11

Advantages and disadvantages of outlines
An outline is a very flexible form of speaking notes. The simplistic layout, with multiple headings and indentations, but with much less text than a written speech, makes an outline

▶ 5.12

---

2   The Times, 29 November 2005.

easy to scan quickly. As a result, you can readily jump around it. If, for example, the judge asks a question about a point that you intend to deal with later in your submissions, you should be able to skip quickly to the relevant section of your notes. Once you have answered the judge's point, you can then launch straight back into your planned submissions without having to find a particular sentence. Greater flexibility also makes time management more straightforward because submissions can easily be curtailed or even dropped.

5.13 ▷ **Figure 5.2:**
Example outline

   I. Introductions
      A. Representing appellant, Charles Dickens
         1. Me
         2. Sydney Carton
      B. Representing respondent, Henry Cecil
         1. Sally Mannering
         2. Roger Thursby
  II. Overview of appeal
      A. First instance
         1. Judge: Steerforth J, QBD
         2. Decision: Dickens gave negligent advice to Cecil re. potential claim by Cecil against firm of accountants, Wickfield's
      B. Grounds of appeal
         1. Dickens owed no duty of care: me
         2. Even if duty of care owed, Dickens did not breach it: Carton

   . . .

As long as it is sufficiently detailed, an outline can also be an excellent prompt. The absence of dense text presents the information that you require in an accessible format that should enable you to lift your eyes from the page frequently. You can then concentrate on engaging the judge eye to eye. Your prompt will also allow you freer rein than a written speech in your choice of words. The "clunkiness" often associated with relying on a script should then be avoided. What is more, with vocabulary to find and arguments to articulate, there is little chance that you will slip into "autopilot" as you might do if you relied on a written speech. You will simply have to concentrate too hard for your mind to wander.

The great drawback of an outline is that it has a low comfort factor. Instead of having a script to work from, you must come up with the words that you speak as you go along. The less detailed your outline, the more thinking you will have to do on your feet. What you gain in spontaneity when all goes well can quickly be lost if one of two disasters strikes. The first is running out of things to say. This phenomenon is not, it should be stressed, confined to mooters who rely on outlines. It is more often a sign of nerves or lack of preparation than of insufficient notes. But there is unquestionably a correlation between the volume of notes and the risk of a protracted pause in a mooter's oral submissions: the fewer the notes, the greater the risk.

The second danger of relying on a sparse outline is the opposite of the first. Without sufficient guidance from your notes, you may start to ramble. Amid the waffle, the judge, and possibly you yourself, may lose the thread of your argument and its persuasive force will accordingly be diminished.

Ad hoc forms of notes

You do not have to choose between drafting a full speech and relying only on an outline. You can instead draft notes that fall somewhere between the two extremes at a place tailored to suit your particular needs.

▶ 5.14

Say, for example, that you like the comfort that a written speech affords, but want to encourage yourself to look up from your notes. You might then write out your speech in full, but capitalise, underline or embolden certain key words or phrases in each sentence. The highlighted sections of your notes would then serve as prompts when you glance at the page, but you could still revert to your script if necessary. You might also insert headings or make liberal use of indentations in your written speech. With the text broken up, you should find it easier to scan quickly.

On the other hand, you might be keen to work from an outline for most of your oral submissions, but wish to leave nothing to chance at certain key points in your speech. You might, for example, be particularly concerned about your opening remarks, because it is relatively easy to become tongue-tied when you start to speak. One solution is to supplement your outline by writing out in full the first few sentences of your submissions. You could take a similar approach elsewhere in your notes. You might, for instance, write out word for word any particularly complicated fact or legal principle to which you will refer.

Figure 5.3:
Example ad hoc notes

▶ 5.15

My Lord,

I appear A = Charles Dickens w/ Sydney Carton

R = Henry Cecil
    − Represented: Sally Mannering & Roger Thursby

Intro.

This is appeal v. decision of Steerforth J. (QBD) that:
    − A gave neg. advice to R
    − Re. pot. claim v. acc, Wickfield's

A appeals on 2 grounds:
    − No DOC to R: me
    − Even if DOC, no breach: Mr Carton

...

Figure 5.3 provides an example of another possible style of ad hoc notes. Like an outline, it makes liberal use of indentations. Where possible, it also uses abbreviated forms of words and initials, two note-reduction techniques that are discussed next in this chapter. Once again, this example covers the opening remarks that appear in longhand in figure 5.1.

Of course, figure 5.3 is only an example of one way in which you might customise your speaking notes. There are many other ad hoc styles, including bullet points and combinations of text and diagrams. You could use any of them, just so long as they work for you on the day of the moot.

TIPS FOR IMPROVING YOUR SPEAKING NOTES

5.16 ▶ Whichever style of speaking notes you adopt, you should constantly be looking for ways to make them more user-friendly. This process is largely a matter of trial and error. If you can learn from watching other people's errors (and other people's trials for that matter), so much the better. What you must be prepared to do is experiment.

The next few pages offer a handful of suggestions for improving the effectiveness of your notes. These ideas should work whether your notes take the form of a written speech, an outline or something altogether different.

Develop note-reduction techniques

5.17 ▶ As a general rule, aim to reduce the length of your speaking notes. The shorter they are, the more manageable they should be; you will be juggling fewer pieces of paper and will consequently be able to find your way around them more easily.

A selection of the devices that you can employ to reduce the length of your notes is described below.

Drop words you can live without

5.18 ▶ Many sentences remain perfectly comprehensible even when the definite and indefinite articles ("the" and "a" or "an"), the words "that" and "which", and most conjunctions (such as "and" and "but") are removed. So take them out. By doing so, you will not only save space, but you will also increase the spontaneity of your submissions because you will not use precisely the same language at the moot as you used when practising your speech beforehand.

Replace words with symbols

5.19 ▶ Symbols can stand in place of certain words. An obvious example is the word "therefore", which is readily comprehensible as "=>". Similarly, the word "paragraph" can be written as "§". There are numerous other possibilities. Some do not greatly reduce the amount of text, but they invariably improve its readability.

Use initials

5.20 ▶ You can drastically shorten the names of particular institutions and certain phrases by initialising the constituent words. You can also initialise individual words. Table 5.4 is a short list of examples, some of which appeared in the ad hoc notes in figure 5.3. You should be able to come up with many more.

Table 5.4:
List of initials

▶ 5.21

Initial(s)	Full version of word(s)
A	appellant
C	claimant
CA	Court of Appeal
ChD	Chancery Division
D	defendant or defender
DOC	duty of care
ECHR	European Court/Convention of/on Human Rights
ECJ	European Court of Justice
HC	High Court
HL	House of Lords
IH	Inner House of the Court of Session
JR	judicial review
OH	Outer House of the Court of Session
P	pursuer
QBD	Queen's Bench Division
R	respondent
SC	Supreme Court
3P	third party

Build a lexicon of abbreviations

Most students develop their own form of shorthand at university as they jot down lecture notes at high speed. It is worth taking the time to develop this skill, not just because it can be put to good use in drafting speaking notes for moots, but because you will use it throughout your professional career. Some of the abbreviations that you adopt may be legal words or phrases, but most will have no specific connection to the law. Every good dictionary contains a list of abbreviations that you can use as a starting point for your lexicon. Table 5.5 provides a few examples. Some are obvious, others hopefully less so.

▶ 5.22

Table 5.5:
List of abbreviations

▶ 5.23

Abbreviation	Full version of word(s)	Abbreviation	Full version of word(s)
a/c	account or accounts	neg	negligence or negligent
acc	accountant	o/	other or over
co	company	opp	opportunity
diff	difference or different	pot	potential
dir	director	ref	reference
est	establish	sol	solicitor
exec	executive	u/	under
gp	group	w/	with
inc	include	wh/	which
		w/o	without

Leave space for supplemental notes

5.24 ▷ However well thought-out your speaking notes may be, you will probably want to supplement them during the moot. There is a good chance, for example, that you will think of several points in rebuttal as you listen to your opponents' submissions. In this event (and plenty of others), you will want to jot down in your notes the points that you wish to make so that you are reminded of them at the appropriate junctures in your speech.

There are many ways of facilitating last-minute additions to your speaking notes. Three are described below:

● **Write notes on loose sheets of paper**

Most mooters make their supplemental notes on additional sheets of paper rather than in the body of their main notes. This approach can work well, but it does lead to a proliferation of paper, which can be difficult to manage as you attempt to flit from main to supplemental notes and back again.

● **Write notes in the margin**

Your margin could extend to as much as half of each page of your notes, although a third might be more workable. You could then make manuscript insertions in the blank part of the page at precisely the point in your notes where you will need them.

● **Write notes on the facing page**

If your speaking notes are written on a medium that leaves you with a blank page facing each page of notes, you can use the blank page for additional points.[3] You might draw arrows from your supplemental notes to the precise spot in your original notes where the new material should be introduced.

Prepare notes for judicial interventions

5.25 ▷ Your notes should not be confined to the submissions that you would make if the judge does not interrupt your speech. You should also draft notes to assist in dealing with the questions that you believe the judge is most likely to ask. If one of those questions comes up, you can turn to your prepared notes and provide a complete and polished response.

As you will not be able to anticipate the precise questions that the judge will ask during your speech, the notes you prepare for dealing with judicial interventions should be in outline or bullet-point form arranged by topic. Not only will you be able to skim-read them more quickly that way, you can also adapt your responses to fit the exact form of the judge's questions.

Supplemental notes of this type are probably best placed at the end of your notes proper or on a separate sheet of paper. You will then have easy access to them if the need arises.

---

[3] Several common media for notes, including two (counsel's notebooks and ring binders) that can be used in this way, are described later in this chapter.

Prepare summaries of the cases you cite

At some point during your oral submissions, and often more than once, you will refer the judge
to a reported case from which you derive a particular legal rule. You may have to provide the
judge with a short and accurate précis of the facts of one or more of these cases. It is therefore
best to prepare case summaries in advance of the moot.

▶ **5.26**

Your summaries need not be long and should focus on the central facts of each reported
decision. Given how familiar you will be with your cited authorities by the time you draft your
speaking notes, producing summaries should not be an onerous task. Since you will not know
precisely when, or even whether, you will need this material, it is again best to include it either
at the end of the main body of your notes or on a separate sheet of paper.

Note the correct form of address for the judge

Mooters sometimes struggle to remember the proper forms of address for judges. You may
therefore find it helpful to write the correct mode of address—usually "My Lady" or "My
Lord"[4]—at the beginning of your speaking notes or even at the top of each page. Some practising advocates follow this approach, particularly when they appear in quick succession before
judges at different levels of the judicial hierarchy who must be addressed in different ways.

▶ **5.27**

MEDIA FOR SPEAKING NOTES

Regardless of the style of speaking notes you use, you will not make best use of them at the
moot if they are written on multiple scraps of paper arranged in no particular order. There are
also few surer ways of removing the veneer of professionalism from a mooting performance
than to rummage around among sheaves of paper for the one crumpled page that contains the
notes for your next submission.

▶ **5.28**

It is therefore vital that you transfer your notes onto a medium that is neat and user-
friendly. There are four main candidates. They are described below in the order of their
popularity in professional practice.

Counsel's notebooks

Few law students would recognise a counsel's notebook. Yet those who go on to appear regularly in court will find within a few years of starting practice that their office shelves are littered
with them. For the uninitiated, counsel's notebooks are like blue school jotters, only taller. They
contain about 50 lined pages of A4 that are perforated on the left-hand side. They are sold by
most large stationers.

▶ **5.29**

Counsel's notebooks offer many advantages as a medium for speaking notes. They are
bound, which means that you will not have to juggle numerous loose pieces of paper. They are
flexible because the perforations allow you to remove pages easily. By virtue of their shape and
suppleness, they are also easy to handle when you are on your feet. You do not, for example,
need a lectern to use them. Perhaps the only significant drawback of counsel's notebooks is
that, unlike certain other media, you cannot insert new pages.

---

4   Ch. 9 explains the correct modes of address for moot judges.

Ring binders

5.30 ▶ The second most prevalent medium for speaking notes in practice is probably the ring binder. The notes themselves are written in manuscript or typed on hole-punched sheets of A4. A few blank pages are often inserted at the end of the file for making notes during the hearing.

Ring binders have many of the attributes of counsel's notebooks. In particular, they keep all of your notes together in one place and they allow you to remove pages. They have the additional benefit that you can insert pages and dividers. The one drawback of ring binders is that they are tricky to manhandle without a lectern. If you choose this medium for your speaking notes and you discover that your moot courtroom is not equipped with a lectern, you are probably best advised to lie the ring binder flat on the table in front of you as you speak rather than attempt to hold it up choirboy-style.

Loose sheets of paper

5.31 ▶ Most mooters use this medium for their speaking notes. Some type their notes. Many write them in manuscript. Although loose sheets of paper are likely to be the most cost-effective and readily available option, they do have drawbacks. If your speaking notes are of the fuller variety, you may be dealing with 10 sheets or more, together, of course, with the moot problem and multiple copies of each of the cited authorities. It is no small task to marshal such a volume of paper when you are addressing a judge.

Even if you take precautions, however, accidents can happen with all that foolscap flying around. The dangers of a mishap can be reduced by stapling the loose sheets together. But it is never easy to deal elegantly with a stapled bundle of papers, particularly as you move backwards and forwards through it when you deal with the judge's interventions.

Cards

5.32 ▶ The great virtue of cards, and the primary reason why they are so prevalent among debaters and best men, is that they are small. They do not therefore flap around and can be held relatively high, enabling speakers to lift their heads and project their voices forward.

What is an undoubted strength in the debating chamber and at wedding receptions is, however, something of a liability in moot courtrooms. Cards simply do not provide sufficient space for the notes that most mooters need. For those who prefer to rely on full speaking notes, the problem is especially acute. They would find themselves clutching a pack of cards thick enough to play poker with.

It is only fair to admit that some mooters use cards very effectively. But you will struggle to find any practising advocates who write their speaking notes on cards. Unless you are already comfortable and confident using cards, you should therefore follow the lead of the professionals and use another medium.

CHAPTER CHECKLIST

- Use a form of speaking notes that suits you.
- Ensure that your speaking notes serve the following functions:
  - An adequate prompt that provides you with the information you require to make flowing submissions.
  - A flexible reference that enables you to adapt to events at the moot.
  - A comfort blanket to which you can retreat if your memory fails you or nerves momentarily overcome you.
- Be aware of, and work to minimise, the drawbacks of the form of speaking notes you use.
- Reduce the length of your speaking notes as much as possible using symbols, abbreviations and initials.
- Leave space in your speaking notes for points that occur to you during the moot.
- Prepare notes of answers to possible questions from the judge and summaries of each case you cite.
- Use a professional-looking and practical medium for your notes, ideally either a counsel's notebook or a ring binder.

▶ 5.33

6
Authorities and bundles

6.1 During your oral submissions, you will take the judge through the authorities on which you rely to support your arguments. You and the judge therefore need to have in front of you hard copies of your chosen reported cases, textbooks and articles. Some moot organisers produce copies of these documents for the judge. But most are not so generous and leave it to the participants to organise. This chapter consequently discusses how to present authorities and provides guidance on preparing bundles.

OPTIONS FOR PRESENTING AUTHORITIES

6.2 There are two well-recognised ways of presenting hard copies of authorities to judges. The first, and most common, is to hand up a copy of each authority during your oral submissions just before you begin to speak about it. The second option is to provide the judge with a "bundle" that contains copies of all the authorities on which you rely. Bundles are typically either handed in to the moot organiser at the same time as the participants exchange lists of authorities and skeleton arguments or they are handed up to the judge at the start of each side's oral submissions during the moot.

The rules of the mooting competition in which you are involved may dictate which of these methods you use. But even if you are not required to prepare a bundle, you should give serious consideration to doing so. They are slightly more expensive to produce than mere photocopies, but well-organised bundles are assets in almost every moot. The judge will have all of your authorities in one, easily accessible place rather than spread randomly across his or her desk. You will also avoid having to interrupt the flow of your oral submissions every time you refer to an authority; instead of proferring yet another sheaf of paper, you can simply refer the judge to a tab or page in your bundle.

Regardless of the method you choose for presenting your authorities to the judge, it is important that you get it right. A sloppy job will distract the judge from what you are trying to say and possibly even cause confusion.

HOW TO PREPARE AUTHORITIES

6.3 Preparing copies of your authorities is not rocket science. All it takes is a little attention to detail. But do not underestimate the importance of that detail. Copying authorities is precisely the sort of task you will be asked to do as a junior lawyer. There are plenty of senior lawyers, possibly even your future bosses, who take the view that trainees and pupils who cannot copy authorities properly are not to be trusted with more challenging, and consequently more interesting, work.

Set out below is a short guide to preparing authorities accurately and professionally. It assumes that you make your copies either by printing them off from an online database or by photocopying bound volumes.

Do not leave it too late

This is the golden rule. If you wait until the last minute before running off copies of your authorities for the judge, you multiply your chances of coming a cropper. The nightmare scenario is that you find the only working computer terminal or photocopier in the law library occupied (by someone other than your mooting partner) and you cannot make any copies at all. Even if you can complete your copying, however, you will be rushed—never the ideal circumstance in which to do a job that requires precision. You will also carry out this mundane task at a time when you should be doing far more important things, like practising your oral submissions.

There should be no need for a last-ditch panic. Most mooting competitions require the participants to exchange lists of authorities at least 24 hours before the moot begins. You should therefore know well in advance of the moot which authorities you have to produce for the judge. Make your copies soon after you finalise your list of authorities.

▶ 6.4

Make sufficient copies

Having gone to the lengths of finding persuasive authorities that support your arguments, ensure you have enough copies to go round at the moot. The classic error is to forget to bring a copy for the judge. Mooters in this position must normally resort to handing up their own copy. They then quickly find that it is very difficult to refer effectively to the important passages of a reported case if they do not have a copy of the decision in front of them.

In order to avoid this fate, produce at least two copies of each of your authorities: one for the judge; and one for you. Follow this practice even if you handed in a bundle of authorities for the judge in advance of the moot. Do not assume that the judge will remember to bring it.

▶ 6.5

Copy the correct version of each case report

As Ch. 4 explained in the context of citing authorities in skeleton arguments, the same case can appear in more than one series of law reports. Make sure that the version you copy is the one you intend to refer to at the moot. It should also, of course, be the version that appears in your list of authorities and any skeleton argument you serve. If you provide the judge with a copy of a different version of a report, you can guarantee confusion all round as you refer during your oral submissions to pages or paragraphs that do not correspond to those in the document the judge is reading.

▶ 6.6

Copy the whole of each case report

Mooters regularly hand up copies of only those pages of case reports to which they intend to refer in their oral submissions. The result is sometimes that 50-page-plus case reports are reduced to as little as two sheets of A4. The motivation for this reductivist tendency is often a

▶ 6.7

laudable desire to protect the environment. But judges usually need to see entire case reports in order to place the passages on which mooters rely in their proper context. As a general rule, you should therefore present the judge with copies of complete reports, including the headnote and every judgment.

Apply common sense, however. You may, for example, wish to refer to a particularly lengthy case report, much of which comprises the arguments of counsel and the judgment of a lower court. In those circumstances, it is usually perfectly appropriate to hand up a truncated version. Precisely what goes into that version will differ in each case, although it should always include the headnote and will almost always include all of the judgments of the senior court. You might take that approach if you wished to rely on *White v Jones*,[1] one of the leading English authorities on duty of care in negligence. The full report is 88 pages long. Rather than copying all of it, you could reasonably limit yourself to the headnote and the speeches of each member of the House of Lords. By omitting the rest, you would reduce your copying to 47 pages. Still a lot, but better than 88.

Copy sufficient pages of textbooks to provide context

6.8 ▶ A different approach is required when you copy extracts from textbooks. As a general rule, copy sufficient pages to give the judge a flavour of the context of the passage on which you rely. In most cases, you will therefore have to copy more than just the page containing the relevant passage, although you should not have to copy more than three or four pages in total. Make sure that the first page of your copy is the title page of the textbook so that the judge can see which book you are citing.

Check each copy you make

6.9 ▶ Get into the habit of reviewing every copy you make as soon as it emerges from the printer or photocopier. Check, in particular, for the following:

● **You have copied every page**
Some photocopiers and printers have a nasty tendency to skip pages, particularly if they are getting low on paper.

● **You have copied the whole of every page**
Ensure that all of the relevant text appears on each page. It is remarkably easy to cut off part of the top, bottom or side of a page, particularly when photocopying long documents.

● **You have not copied any page squint**
When photocopying from a hard-copy textbook or law report, the text can appear on the copy at an angle if the book is not carefully positioned on the copier.

● **You have arranged every page in the correct order**
Before you fasten your copies together, ensure that all of the pages follow consecutively and that you have not inadvertently re-arranged them.

---

[1] [1995] 2 A.C. 207.

Checking your copies to this level of detail takes time, but it is imperative if you are to avoid embarrassment and confusion at the moot.

Use one sheet for each page of text

Unless the competition rules say otherwise, each sheet of your copies should contain only one page of text. You should therefore avoid printing on both sides of each sheet or printing two pages of text on a single side of each sheet. Similarly, do not produce copies of authorities on which the text is so small that it is virtually illegible to anyone with less than 20/20 vision. If anything, you should veer towards enlarging the text.

▶ 6.10

Do not mark your copies

Best practice is to hand up to the judge clean copies of your authorities. If the judge wants to mark them in some way, he or she will do so prior to or during the moot. Do not therefore present authorities pre-highlighted and on no account hand up authorities with manuscript annotations.

▶ 6.11

Fasten your copies (except in bundles)

If you are handing up authorities one by one, each copy you present should be individually fastened, preferably with a staple. If the authority is too long to be stapled, fasten it in some other way, such as with a bulldog clip or treasury tag (a piece of string with metal-covered ends). Avoid paper clips as they tend not to keep documents securely fastened for long. But even paper clips are better than nothing.

▶ 6.12

If you are providing a bundle, your authorities will automatically be secure and will not need further fastening. You should therefore insert them into the bundle in loose-leaf form. If each authority is fastened, the judge will probably have to take it out of the bundle in order to read it. Some of the benefit of using a bundle will then be lost.

A final flip through

When you have followed all of this advice and have in front of you a neat stack or bundle of authorities, flick through them one last time. Make sure that every authority is present and correct.

▶ 6.13

ADDITIONAL CONSIDERATIONS SPECIFIC TO BUNDLES

Professional lawyers are subject to detailed rules about the preparation and contents of bundles, as well as strict deadlines by which they must lodge bundles in court.[2] As a mooter, you will not be so constrained. Nonetheless, whether you prepare a bundle on your own initiative or because you are bound (as it were) by the competition rules, there are a few things you should know about how to do it.

▶ 6.14

---

[2] For examples of the rules that apply in England, see paras 3.1 to 3.10 of Practice Direction 39A of the CPR and Appendix 6 of the Chancery Guide.

Contents

6.15 ▶ Most well-presented bundles contain the following documents in the following order:

● **Index**
The index appears at the start of the bundle. It should include the name of the moot problem and identify the party on whose behalf the bundle is served. It should then list the contents of the bundle in the order in which they appear. Each authority should be given its full citation.

● **Skeleton argument**
If you have prepared a skeleton argument, it is usually a good idea to include a copy in the bundle immediately after the index.

● **Authorities**
Insert a copy of each authority that your team included in its list of authorities for exchange with the other side. Your authorities should be arranged in the order in which they appear in your skeleton argument or, if you have not served one, in the order in which you will refer to the authorities during your oral submissions at the moot.

Internal format

6.16 ▶ A bundle containing all of the right documents in the right order will not look professional if it is not presented properly. To achieve this end, follow the guidelines below when you collate the documents for your bundle:

● **Separate each document**
Place each document in the bundle behind a divider or some other means of separation (such as coloured plastic "post-it" notes). Otherwise, the judge may have to flick through the entire bundle each time he or she has to locate a particular authority.

● **Paginate the bundle**
If your bundle is not too long, insert sequential numbers in manuscript at the bottom of each page. Pagination can speed up references to authorities during your oral submissions. Rather than referring the judge to a tab in the bundle and then to a page number of the document within the tab, you can simply ask the judge to "please turn to page [X] of the bundle".

● **Hole-punch carefully**
When you hole-punch documents for your bundle, make sure that you insert the holes in the same place on each page. Deviation from this practice will leave the edges of your authorities looking like badly folded newspapers.

External format

6.17 ▶ Your bundle should appear professional not only on the inside, but also on the outside. There are two particular considerations to bear in mind concerning the external format of bundles:

● **Binding**

You have several options for binding your documents together. The option you choose will probably come down to personal preference and the resources at your disposal. All that really matters is that the pages are securely contained, but sufficiently accessible to enable the judge to read them easily. Comb binding (which binds documents together using a plastic spine with "teeth") and wire spiral binding are both perfectly good techniques, although you will need access to the necessary equipment. Treasury tags are also fine. Best of all is a ring binder. It looks professional and is user-friendly. You should also be able to use ring binders more than once because judges will usually return bundles if so requested.

● **Labelling**

If both sides serve bundles, the judge will want to see at a glance whose bundle is whose. You should therefore attach labels to the spine and front of the bundle. The labels should identify the name of the moot problem and the party on whose behalf the bundle has been prepared.

CHAPTER CHECKLIST

▶ 6.18

- Prepare a bundle of authorities if you can.
- If you prepare a bundle:
  - Include an index, your skeleton argument (if you have prepared one) and a copy of each authority on which your team relies.
  - Separate each document in the bundle, preferably with a divider.
  - Number each page consecutively unless the bundle is particularly long.
  - Place the documents in a professional-looking and user-friendly form of binding that is clearly labelled.
- Whether or not you prepare a bundle:
  - Make copies of all of your authorities in good time for the moot.
  - Make two copies of your authorities: one for the judge and one for you.
  - Copy the whole of each case report unless there is a good reason for not doing so.
  - Copy each page of text onto a single sheet of paper.
  - Make sure that your copies are readable and complete.
  - Do not write on or highlight any of the copies you give to the judge.

▶ 7
Practice

7.1 ▶ Practising oral submissions is a vital part of preparing for moots, particularly for those who have not mooted before. The more you practise, and the more effective your practising is, the more polished and persuasive your submissions will be. You should therefore carve out sufficient time to practise your submissions, however busy you are in the build-up to the moot.

This chapter is divided into two parts: the first identifies the main benefits of practising oral submissions; the second describes several methods of going about it.

BENEFITS OF PRACTICE

7.2 ▶ If your practice regimen is limited to a quick read through your notes on the morning of the moot, you will not be as prepared as you should be for your oral submissions. Practising your speech properly offers several key benefits. They are outlined below.

Gain familiarity with your submissions

7.3 ▶ Whether you rely on a full written speech or minimal notes, practising your submissions will help you to remember them. That is not to say that you should set out to memorise your submissions word for word, although you may find that you do so naturally as you practise them. It is rather that you want to be familiar with your submissions so that you are not overly tied to the page when you speak and can consequently make regular eye contact with the judge. Practising your submissions will also familiarise you with your speaking notes and enable you to find specific information in a hurry at the moot.

Anticipate the judge's questions

7.4 ▶ As you practise your submissions, you can think about the questions the judge might ask. If you practise in front of other people, encourage them to do likewise. This aspect of practice can be critical. When he was still an attorney, Thurgood Marshall, the former United States Supreme Court justice, famously practised his oral argument for the seminal race-relations case *Brown v Board of Education* in front of several law students the day before the hearing. One of the students asked a question that had Marshall stumped. He worked up an answer overnight. The next day, one of the judges asked the very same question. Marshall had a ready reply.

Adjust the length of your speech

If you time your submissions while you practise them, you can adjust their length so that they ▶ 7.5 neither exceed your allotted speaking time nor leave any time unutilised. Given that your speaking slot at the moot will be relatively short, you must time your submissions accurately. If possible, use a stopwatch and time your submissions more than once so that you can check for consistency. You should also time yourself in circumstances that replicate actual mooting conditions. The following tips should help you do so:

● **Practise with your papers**

Practise using all of the papers you will have to marshal at the moot. You will lose time whenever you move from one sheet of paper to another. Build that delay into your timing.

● **Take account of time lost when you refer to authorities**

You will also lose time whenever you refer the judge to one of your authorities. However dexterous your judge might be, he or she will inevitably need a few seconds to find the right page and paragraph. You will have to halt your submissions in the meantime. Factor this hiatus into your timing.

● **Allow time for the judge's questions**

The rules of your mooting competition should stipulate whether or not the clock stops running when the judge asks questions. If it does not stop, you must allow sufficient time in your oral submissions, perhaps two or three minutes, for dealing with judicial interventions. Take that time into account when you practise.

After timing your submissions, you may find it helpful to record in your notes a few key "milestones" that you can use during the moot to gauge the pace of your delivery. For example, you might mark the point in your notes (perhaps by making a small notation in the margin) when you expect to reach the halfway point in your allotted speaking time. If, as you are delivering your oral submissions at the moot, you pass this juncture sooner than expected, you will know to slow down or include an extra point. On the other hand, if it takes you longer to get to this marker than it did when you practised, you may have to skip a point.

Improve delivery

Practising your oral submissions should improve your delivery in several ways. As you ▶ 7.6 become more familiar with your submissions, you will speak with a more natural voice. Repeated practice should also help you to identify any potentially distracting verbal habits or physical mannerisms. Some people are prone, for example, to repeating particular words and phrases without realising it. Common offenders include the words "basically" and "like", and the phrases "you know" and "I mean". Other people have a tendency to clear their throats with unnatural regularity. Yet others play with their earlobes or twiddle pens in their fingers. All of these idiosyncrasies can be spotted and ironed out as you practise your submissions.

Polish your speaking notes

7.7 ▶ Practising your submissions will enable you to improve your speaking notes. If you have drafted a fullish speech, practising it should highlight any clumsy phraseology, which you can then amend. If you have drafted more truncated notes, running through your submissions should tell you whether they provide the prompts that you need in order to remember the points you wish to make. Any notes that are insufficient for that purpose can be supplemented accordingly.

Build confidence

7.8 ▶ The more you practise your submissions, the more confident you are likely to feel at the moot. You will be more conversant with your notes and will therefore be less worried about losing your place. You will know your arguments better too and should consequently feel more able to defend them.

HOW TO PRACTISE

Specific methods

7.9 ▶ You can practise your submissions in a variety of ways. Five of the most common and effective are described below. Use as many of them as you can as often as you are able. It is very hard to practise too much.

Practising out loud on your own

7.10 ▶ This method is probably most people's idea of practising their submissions. It involves running through your oral submissions in the speaking voice you will adopt at the moot. You may feel a little self-conscious when you practise in this way, even if you lock yourself in your bedroom and stay well out of earshot of anyone else. But it is hugely valuable, particularly for timing your submissions, committing them to memory and working on your delivery.

    Another helpful feature of speaking out loud is that it accustoms you to the sound of your own voice. Many law students are only too familiar with (and enamoured of) the lilt and cadence of their own voices, but there are others who have not had the benefit of listening to themselves speaking regularly in public. This form of practice will acquaint them with how they sound.

Practising in front of a mirror

7.11 ▶ You can take practising out loud a step farther by standing in front of a mirror while you speak. What you will gain from this, apparently narcissistic, exercise is a very clear idea of whether you know your submissions well enough to make frequent eye contact with the judge. If you can look yourself steadily in the eyes for long periods as you speak, you should be able to do the same thing to the judge.

    Practising your submissions in front of a mirror can also highlight mannerisms that might not otherwise be apparent to you. You are likely to obtain the greatest benefit from this form of practice if you use a full-length mirror that allows you to watch your whole body.

Practising in front of someone else

7.12 ▶ Ideally, you should practise your oral submissions for each moot at least once in front of someone else, preferably your mooting partner (if you have one). Practice of this type will provide an objective assessment of your performance. An observer will give you valuable feedback about the persuasiveness of your arguments and will spot any distracting physical or verbal habits.

As explained above, your audience should not be passive, but should intervene with questions of the type that the judge might ask at the moot. Such an audience will give you an opportunity to practise responding to judicial interventions (remember Thurgood Marshall) and, in the process, to skip around your speaking notes. You will then not only become more familiar with your notes, you will also have a more accurate sense of how long your submissions are likely to last.

Practising with audio and video equipment

If you have access to audio or video equipment, including a smart phone, you may learn a great deal from recording your performance. Listening to yourself can be quite a disconcerting experience. Your voice may sound very different from how you imagine it. The experience can be useful, however, particularly as it will ruthlessly highlight your "ums" and "errs", as well as any words and phrases that you employ with irritating regularity. ▶ 7.13

If listening to your voice is enlightening, seeing yourself on video is even more so. As long as you can deal with the cringe factor, watching yourself on screen not only provides a good appreciation of what you look and sound like on your feet, but also gives a sense of how engaging you are as a speaker. You will see very quickly whether you look as though you are reading a speech and you will spot problems with your stance and delivery. You may discover that you appear far more accomplished than you felt while running through your speech. That realisation will provide a welcome confidence boost.

Practising in silence

By far the easiest way of practising your submissions is to go over them in your head. You might, for example, carry a copy of your speaking notes around with you, read a line or two when you have a spare moment and then try to continue the submission without looking again at your notes. This form of practice is best used for committing oral submissions to memory and familiarising yourself with the layout of your notes. ▶ 7.14

You can also contemplate silently the interventions that the judge might make during your oral submissions. The more you play around with ideas in your head, the more likely you are to anticipate the focus of the judge's questions and to develop plausible answers to them.

The beauty of practising submissions in silence is that you can do it virtually anywhere and at almost any time. You can even do it on public transport. Just make sure that you do not move your lips too much or your fellow travellers may start to question your sanity.

Be warned, however, that if you only practise silently you may be under-prepared. Speaking out loud is a very different beast from silent practice, not least because the former is a much slower process. Always therefore practise out loud at least once before each moot.

General points

Whichever practice methods you use, aim to get the most out of them. You are more likely to do so if you follow the steps described below. ▶ 7.15

Make your practice authentic

7.16 ▶ Most mooters practise their submissions at home. There is nothing wrong with that. But if you can run through your speech at least once in the actual moot courtroom or a room like it, the experience will be considerably more authentic and, consequently, more helpful.

Maximising authenticity also involves speaking in the body position that you will adopt at the moot. Almost invariably, you will have to deliver your oral submissions standing up. So practise them in that position, and not lounging on the sofa with a drink in your hand.

Look up regularly

7.17 ▶ The more eye contact you have with the judge, the more effective your oral submissions will be. You should therefore use your practice sessions to test how often you can lift your eyes from the page. If you lose your place in your speaking notes now and again, it does not matter. Try to "ad lib" a few sentences. If you are struggling to look up regularly, perhaps because you are working from a full written speech, memorise a few key passages and practise delivering them with your head held high.

Think about the substance of your submissions

7.18 ▶ Even though you will practise your submissions relatively close to the moot (most likely, the night before or the morning of) it is not too late to tinker with the substance of your arguments. As you practise, you should therefore keep a weather eye on the persuasiveness of what you are saying. You may find one or two points that looked convincing on paper, but sound hollow when you express them out loud.

CHAPTER CHECKLIST

7.19 ▶
- Practise your oral submissions as many times as possible.
- The most common and effective methods of practice are as follows:
  - Speaking out loud on your own.
  - Speaking in front of someone else.
  - Recording yourself using audio or video equipment.
  - Practising silently.
- Always practise out loud on your own at least once.
- Ideally, practise at least once in front of someone who asks you questions.
- Make your practice as authentic as you can.

Appearing

"One junior rose—with eyeballs tense,
And swollen frontal veins:
To all his powers of eloquence
He gave the fullest reins."

W S Gilbert, English dramatist and librettist (1836–1911)

▶ 8
Preliminaries

For the uninitiated, a moot courtroom must seem a bit like a foreign country. It has a distinctive geography, it has its own set of customs and it is populated by not altogether friendly natives. If you are about to appear in your first moot, it will therefore pay dividends to spend a little time planning your trip before you leave home. This chapter aims to provide your preparatory reading. It advises you when to travel to the moot, explains what you should bring with you and describes what you should find when you reach the moot courtroom. Think of this chapter as a *Lonely Planet Guide* for novice mooters.

▶ 8.1

GETTING TO THE MOOT

Even if you do not have far to travel, always set out for the moot courtroom in time to arrive at least 15 minutes before the moot is due to begin. If you cut your timing too fine, you are likely to arrive flushed, flustered and a bag of nerves.

▶ 8.2

Arriving at the moot courtroom in good time does not mean that you are obliged to wait for an eternity outside, twiddling your thumbs or engaging in that rather false bonhomie that often precedes moots, exams and other such occasions. You may wish to do so, of course. If not, you can usefully take one of two courses. The first is to go into the moot courtroom, sit in your seat and ready yourself for the moot. You may end up sitting for quite a long time, but you can sensibly use it to discuss any last-minute points with your mooting partner (assuming he or she has also turned up early).

The alternative approach is to repair to a quiet spot within a short distance of the moot courtroom, possibly a nearby classroom, and remain there until a few minutes before the moot is scheduled to start. You can arrange to meet your mooting partner at this location and use the period before the moot begins to run over your oral submissions one last time.

WHAT TO BRING TO THE MOOT

Mooters, like junior lawyers, must bring a considerable amount of paraphernalia to court. In the heated build-up to a moot, it is easy to forget something. It is therefore worth compiling a list and gathering together everything on it before you leave home.

▶ 8.3

Set out below is a checklist of the items that every mooter should normally take to each moot. Those items marked with an asterisk are essential; the remainder are matters of personal preference.

● **Your speaking notes***

● **One copy of the moot problem***

● **Two copies of your skeleton argument***
One copy is for you and the other is for the judge in case he or she did not receive your skeleton argument before the moot or (perish the thought) forgot to bring it along. There is obviously no need for both you and your mooting partner to bring a spare copy of your skeleton for the judge.

● **One copy of your opponents' skeleton argument***

● **Two copies of each of your authorities***
Again, one of these copies is for your use during the moot and the other is for the judge. As explained in Ch.6, it is sensible to take a spare copy for the judge even if you have provided a bundle of authorities in advance of the moot because there is always a risk that the judge has not received it or has mislaid it.

● **One copy of each of your opponents' authorities***
It is for your opponents to ensure that the judge has copies of their authorities. You do not therefore need a spare, just one for yourself.

● **A pen***

● **A second pen***
In case your first pen packs up during the moot.

● **A highlighter**
Highlighters are very handy for marking authorities, particularly those passages on which your opponents rely or that the judge identifies as important.

● **Spare sheets of paper for making notes during the moot[1]**

● **"Post-it" notes**
"Post-it" notes enable you to identify easily particular documents or parts of documents. They are also useful for conveying short messages to your mooting partner during the moot.

With all of this clobber to carry, it will be a wonder if you have room in your bag for anything else. But if you do, avoid the temptation to pack a good luck charm and display it on your table in the moot courtroom. Battered teddy bears and pink gonks used to be *de rigueur* on *University Challenge*, but they are incompatible with the air of confident professionalism that you are endeavouring to create at a moot. If you really must bring a furry friend, keep him or her (or it) well away from public view.

---

[1] An alternative to having separate sheets of paper is to create space within your speaking notes. Ch. 5 discusses the format of notes in detail.

LAYOUT OF MOOT COURTROOMS

Moot courtrooms vary tremendously from institution to institution. The grander exam- ▶ 8.4
ples are almost indistinguishable from real courts, coming fully equipped with witness stands,
jury boxes and microphones. The majority of moot courtrooms are less imposing, however,
often being nothing more than working classrooms with the furniture re-arranged.

Whether grand or humble, moot courtrooms are usually laid out in the same way. This
standard configuration mimics the arrangement of real courts. Figure 8.1 illustrates the typical
layout of an English moot courtroom. It shows the moot court clerk sitting to the right of the
judge(s), but he or she might just as readily sit to the left or even in front of the judge(s).

Figure 8.1: ▶ 8.5
Typical layout of an English moot courtroom

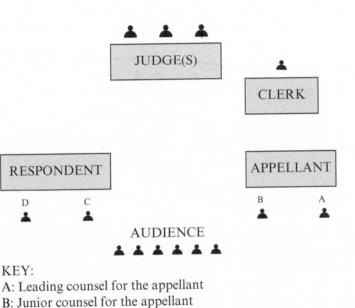

KEY:
A: Leading counsel for the appellant
B: Junior counsel for the appellant
C: Leading counsel for the respondent
D: Junior counsel for the respondent

Scottish moot courtrooms look different from their English counterparts, reflecting the
layout of real courts in Scotland. Figure 8.2 illustrates the typical Scottish arrangement.

The standard layouts of moot courtrooms in England and Scotland accommodate the
judge (or judges), the mooters, the moot court clerk and the audience. The typical seating
arrangements for all of these people are discussed in more detail below.

8.6 ▶ **Figure 8.2:**
Typical layout of a Scottish moot courtroom

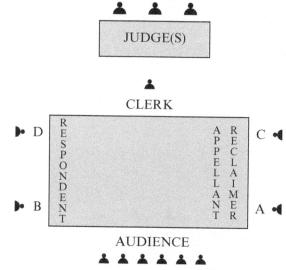

KEY:
A: Junior counsel for the appellant/reclaimer
B: Junior counsel for the respondent
C: Senior counsel for the appellant/reclaimer
D: Senior counsel for the respondent

Judge(s)

8.7 ▶ The moot judge sits at the front of the moot courtroom at the "bench". In the better-appointed moot courtrooms, the bench consists of a fixed wooden desk with sufficient space to accommodate up to three judges sitting line abreast. Very often, this desk is on a raised platform, enabling the judges to look down from their lofty perch on the mooters below. In more modest moot courtrooms, the bench is no more than a table or two sitting at the same level as the rest of the furniture.

Mooters

8.8 ▶ The mooters sit at a table or tables in front of the bench. Looking from the back of the moot courtroom, the mooters appearing for the appellant (or reclaimer) sit on the right and those for the respondent sit on the left. As figures 8.1 and 8.2 show, whereas in England each team generally sits at its own table facing forward, in Scotland there is usually one central table at which both teams sit opposite each other.

    Some mooting competitions make lecterns available to mooters. The lectern may be fixed and positioned an equal distance between the two teams. More commonly, a portable lectern is placed on the table or tables at which the mooters sit. In that event, when each mooter finishes speaking, he or she is expected to pass the lectern to the next mooter to address the court.

Moot court clerk

Not every mooting competition employs a moot court clerk. When they are used, however, they either sit slightly to one side of the bench or, if the judge is seated on a raised dais, directly in front of the judge. The moot court clerk is usually provided with a desk on which to rest papers and any equipment for timing the mooters' submissions. ▶ 8.9

Audience

The "public gallery" sits at the back of most moot courtrooms. The spectators typically sit in rows that start a few feet behind the mooters' chairs. ▶ 8.10

CHAPTER CHECKLIST

- Arrive at the moot courtroom at least 15 minutes before the moot is due to begin. ▶ 8.11
- Use the time before the moot starts to talk with your mooting partner and, possibly, practise your speeches.
- Take with you to the moot as a minimum the items marked with an asterisk on the list contained in this chapter.
- Remember the standard layout of moot courtrooms in your jurisdiction and sit in the right place.

▶ 9
Etiquette

9.1 ▶ Mooters must observe certain rules of etiquette. Moots are not university-union-style debates, but mock court hearings. To be as realistic as possible, moots must therefore assume some of the solemnity of real court proceedings. The rules of mooting etiquette play a vital role in creating the requisite atmosphere of civility and professionalism.

Mooting etiquette can be a source of irritation and confusion for students. The purpose of this chapter is to steer you through the minefield. To that end, this chapter describes the main rules relating to mooters' attire, the proper forms of address for judges and fellow mooters, and the circumstances in which you should stand and sit during moots. It ends with some general guidance on modern mooting manners. If the last chapter was a *Lonely Planet Guide* for novice mooters, this chapter is a mooters' *Debrett's*.

DRESS

9.2 ▶ Your attire — what you wear — is possibly the most important aspect of moot court etiquette. Most judges will forgive the odd verbal slip-up when you address them, but many come down hard on mooters who look shabby.

Some students take exception to dressing up to moot. They may feel self-conscious or uncomfortable out of their jeans. The rationale for dressing up is therefore outlined below. There follows a guide on how to dress at moots and an explanation of when the mooting dress code applies.

Why dress up?

9.3 ▶ What you wear impacts not only the judge's impression of you, but the way in which you yourself behave. Observing the mooting dress code produces the following specific benefits:

● **You will impress the judge**
Dressing properly will create a positive impression on the judge. The most pernickety moot judges in this regard are often those who are members of the judiciary in real life. Their attitude may be partly explained by their keener awareness of the need for advocates to show respect to the court. But they also doubtless appreciate, from many years of sitting in court, that untidy advocates all too often produce untidy arguments.

● **Your dress will not distract the judge**

If you wear much the same attire as every other mooter, the judge will not be distracted by your appearance and will find it easy to concentrate on what you say. By contrast, the judge will struggle to follow your oral submissions if you deliver them dressed in a tee shirt emblazoned with the latest legend from French Connection ("I love mcok courts", perhaps).

● **You will look professional**

Mooting is modelled on professional practice. Even with the advent of "dress-down Fridays" at many law firms and barristers' chambers, most lawyers still wear suits for the bulk of the working week. If mooters want to look like legal professionals, they must dress like them.

● **You will feel professional**

If you dress like a professional lawyer, you will feel the part. If you feel like a professional lawyer, you are more likely to act like one.

● **You will get used to wearing suits**

As an aspiring professional, you need to feel and look comfortable in suits. Even before you start work (in a suit-dominated office), you will likely have to attend several job interviews. In a suit. You will find it hard to make a good impression with interviewers if you shuffle and fidget in unfamiliar garb.

What should you wear?

When deciding what to wear to a moot, first check the competition rules. They may incorporate a dress code. In the absence of specific guidance from the rules, assume that you are required to wear business attire or the nearest thing to it that you can manage. No-one will expect you to buy a suit especially for a moot, but you will be expected to dress smartly (or, as the English Bar Council's guidance puts it, "decorously"). For the avoidance of doubt, a short guide is provided below. ▶ 9.4

Men

- A two- or three- piece suit, preferably in navy, charcoal grey or black. Failing that, a pair of smart trousers in a dark colour or khaki, and a jacket. ▶ 9.5
- A collared shirt, ideally in white or a mild shade of a neutral colour such as blue or pink. Conservative patterns, such as thin stripes, are acceptable too.
- A tie. Avoid anything too garish. The judge should not be treated to one of your hilarious ties from the Homer Simpson neckwear collection.
- A clean pair of smart shoes. You will ruin the effect you are trying to create if you turn up at the moot in a scruffy pair of trainers.

Women

- A skirt- or trouser-suit, preferably in black, navy or dark grey. If you do not own a suit, wear a skirt or a pair of trousers with a jacket. Skirts should be at least knee-length. ▶ 9.6

- A business-style shirt. The same principles apply to colours and patterns for women's shirts as to men's.
- A pair of smart shoes. Heels are fine, but remember that you will have to stand for fairly long periods while you make your oral submissions. The six-inch stilettos should probably therefore stay at home.

Wearing gowns

9.7 ▶ In order to inject greater realism into the proceedings, some mooting competitions require the competitors to wear gowns. Gowns are not the most user-friendly garments. Wear one that is too small and you run the risk of looking like Alice in Wonderland after drinking the potion that made her grow. If your gown is too large, the sleeves may get in the way when you handle your papers and the whole garment may slip off your back as you deliver your submissions. A super-sized gown may even lodge itself under your chair when you sit down, thereby guaranteeing an embarrassing commotion when you try to stand up again. Given the inconvenience that ill-fitting gowns can cause, make sure you wear one that fits.

When does the dress code apply?

9.8 ▶ Unless you are told otherwise, the dress code applies whenever you are in the moot courtroom and not just when you are on your feet making submissions to the judge. Do not therefore arrive at the moot in trainers and proceed to change into a smarter pair of shoes when one of your opponents is addressing the court. Nor should you take off your jacket or loosen your tie once you have finished your speech. Maintain your standard of dress even when you return to the moot courtroom to receive the judge's verdict (however refreshing any interval drinks may have been).

FORMS OF ADDRESS

9.9 ▶ Few matters of moot court etiquette cause more trouble than the modes of address that students are supposed to adopt when they refer to judges and fellow mooters. The required forms of address are old-fashioned and sound odd to the unpractised ear, but you need to master them if you are to avoid looking and feeling awkward and inexperienced. This section describes the proper forms of address.

The moot judge

9.10 ▶ The British courts employ a plethora of forms of address for judges at different levels of the judicial hierarchy.[1] As a result, junior practitioners sometimes fail to refer to judges accurately, particularly if they appear in quick succession before tribunals that should be addressed in different ways. Thankfully, the task of addressing moot judges is relatively straightforward because English and Scottish moots take place in courts where the judges are addressed in the same way.[2] Table 9.1 contains the proper forms of address for moot judges.

---

[1]   For a comprehensive list of the correct forms of address for members of each level of the judiciary of England and Wales, go to *www.judiciary.gov.uk* and click the link entitled "What is the right way to address a judge?"

[2]   As Ch.2 explains, those courts are the Court of Appeal and the Supreme Court in England and Wales, and the Inner House of the Court of Session and the High Court of Justiciary in Scotland.

Table 9.1:
Forms of address for moot judges

▶ 9.11

Tribunal	"Direct" form of address	Form of address in place of "you"	Form of address in place of "your"
Single male judge	"My Lord"	"Your Lordship"	"Your Lordship's"
Single female judge	"My Lady"	"Your Ladyship"	"Your Ladyship's"
All-male panel of judges	Collectively: "My Lords"	Collectively: "Your Lordships"	Collectively: "Your Lordships'"
	Individually: "My Lord"	Individually: "Your Lordship"	Individually: "Your Lordship's"
All-female panel of judges	Collectively: "My Ladies"	Collectively: "Your Ladyships"	Collectively: "Your Ladyships'"
	Individually: "My Lady"	Individually: "Your Ladyship"	Individually: "Your Ladyship's"
Mixed-sex panel of judges	Collectively: "My Lords"	Collectively: "Your Lordships"	Collectively: "Your Lordships'"
	Individually: "My Lord" or "My Lady" as appropriate	Individually: "Your Lordship" or "Your Ladyship" as appropriate	Individually: "Your Lordship's" or "Your Ladyship's" as appropriate

The second column of table 9.1 shows the proper forms of address when speaking to judges directly (i.e., when you would in normal conversation use his or her name). For example, you might say as follows:

● *"My Lord, I appear on behalf of the respondent in this appeal."*
● *"It is submitted, My Ladies, that the leading case in this area of the law is . . ."*

The third and fourth columns of table 9.1 show the proper forms of address when you would use the words "you" and "your" respectively in normal conversation. Neither "you" nor "your" is appropriate when addressing a judge. For example, you might say as follows:

● *"Would Your Ladyships please turn to page two of the respondent's skeleton argument?"*
● *"If I understand Your Lordship's point correctly, . . ."*

There is nothing to stop you from combining more than one form of address in a single sentence. You might therefore say this, for example:

● *"My Lord, I would now like to deal in more detail with the point Your Lordship mentioned a moment ago."*

When you start mooting, you will find these forms of address rather cumbersome and you will trip up occasionally. It is particularly easy to place a "My Lord/Lady" where a "Your Lordship/Ladyship" should go, or to address incorrectly a tribunal that consists of more than one judge. As you gain in experience, however, you will find that addressing judges properly becomes almost second nature.

Judges other than the moot judge

9.12 ▶ In the course of your oral submissions, you are likely to refer to several judges other than the moot judge. You will almost certainly mention the fictitious lower court judge who appears in the moot problem and whose decision you are seeking to uphold or overturn. You will also refer to the real-life judges whose reported decisions you rely on as authorities.

The titles of some British judges are pronounced differently in court from the way in which they appear in writing. You therefore need to know how to pronounce them properly. Table 9.2 lists some of the most common judicial titles in written form with the correct pronunciation next to each.

9.13 ▶ **Table 9.2:**
Forms of address for other judges

Written	**Spoken**
Smith HHJ	"His/Her Honour Judge Smith"
Smith J	"Mr/Mrs Justice Smith"
Smith LJ	"Lord/Lady Justice Smith"
Smith and Jones LJJ	"Lord/Lady Justices Smith and Jones"
Lord Smith of Smithfield	"Lord Smith"
Lady Smith of Smithfield	"Lady Smith"

A final point on referring to judges other than the moot judge: however senior or junior the judge may be, the convention is to refer to him or her as "the learned judge". Thus, for example, you might start your oral submissions in this way:

- *"This is an appeal against the decision of Mr Justice Smith. The learned judge held that . . ."*

Your opponents

9.14 ▶ You are likely to refer to your opponents quite often during your oral submissions. If you are the first mooter to speak, you will introduce them. Whenever you refute one of their points, you will also mention them. There are various acceptable formulations for referring to your opponents. Most of them are listed below:

- *"My learned friend"*
- *"My learned friend, Mr/Ms [??]"*
- *"My learned friend opposite"*

- *"Leading/junior counsel for the appellant/respondent"*
- *"Mr/Ms [??]"*

It is never appropriate to refer to an opponent by his or her first name.

Your mooting partner

Whenever you refer to your team-mate during your oral submissions, whether in the course of introducing the mooters to the judge or otherwise, refer to him or her using one of the following forms: ▶ 9.15

- *"My learned friend"*
- *"My learned friend, Mr/Ms [??]"*
- *"My learned junior/leader"*
- *"Mr/Ms [??]"*

Again, never use your mooting partner's first name.

STANDING UP AND SITTING DOWN

A recognised protocol governs when mooters should stand in moot courtrooms and when they should sit. As ever, this protocol replicates the rules that apply in real courts. ▶ 9.16

Start of the moot

You will usually be seated in the moot courtroom before the judge arrives. When he or she enters the room, you should stand. The moot court clerk, if there is one, will usually prompt those assembled with the words, "Court rise". On reaching his or her seat, the judge will normally give a small bow of the head before sitting down. You should bow in similar fashion before also sitting down. ▶ 9.17

Occasionally, the judge will already be seated at the bench when you enter the moot courtroom at the start of the moot. In that event, walk to your seat and bow. Then sit down when the judge invites you to do so.

During the moot

Always stand when you address the judge unless he or she tells you otherwise. Only sit down once you have completed your oral submissions and the judge has indicated that no further assistance is required from you (which judges often do by simply saying, "Thank you"). ▶ 9.18

It is rare in moots for a judge to invite a mooter to say something during another mooter's speech. If that happens, however, the non-speaking mooter should immediately stand and deal with the judge's question. The mooter who was speaking should meanwhile sit down and only stand up again when the exchange between the judge and the new speaker has finished.

Non-speaking mooters should remain seated unless the judge addresses a question directly to them. Moots are unlike debates in that you cannot jump to your feet and make points of information or points of order. Nor can you holler, "Objection!" as American attorneys do. If you disagree with what your opponents are saying, make a note of their point. You or your mooting partner can then deal with it in your oral submissions.

End of the moot

9.19 ▶ Once both sides have completed their oral submissions, the judge will probably leave the moot courtroom to consider the verdict. When the judge stands at the end of the moot, you should stand too. Before moving off, the judge will often bow. If so, follow suit. Then remain standing until the judge has left the room. If, as sometimes happens, the judge remains in the moot courtroom to deliberate, the mooters should stand, bow their heads in the judge's direction and leave the room.

GOOD MANNERS

9.20 ▶ It would be going too far to say that manners maketh the mooter, but bad manners can certainly maketh a poor impression on the judge. If the judge forms a bad impression of you, your credibility will be damaged and the judge will have more sympathy for your opponents.

Displaying good manners during a moot involves nothing more than observing common courtesies. Principal among them are the following:

● **Turn off your mobile phone**
There are few things more likely to induce apoplexy in a judge than the ring tone of a mobile phone. Turn your mobile off before you enter the moot courtroom and do not switch it back on until after the moot has finished.

● **Do not interrupt the judge**
If the judge intervenes during your oral submissions, do not interrupt the question even if you see where it is going. Wait until the judge finishes the point before you start to answer it.

● **Do not leave the moot courtroom**
Unless an emergency arises, remain at your seat in the moot courtroom for the duration of the moot. The judge will be disconcerted, distracted and probably annoyed by the spectacle of a mooter coming and going while the court is "in session".

● **Stay silent during your opponents' submissions**
You may disagree vehemently with what your opponents are saying, but that is no excuse for engaging in theatrical bouts of paper shuffling, coughs, tuts, sharp intakes of breath, titters, yawns, sighs or grunts. Your opponents are entitled to make their points (as are you) without an attendant cacophony of farmyard noise.

● **Pay attention to your team-mate's submissions**
There is no need to gaze adoringly on your team-mate during his or her oral submissions. You are not a Tory politician watching your leader address the party conference. Just make sure that you are (and look as if you are) actively following what is being said. Not only is your team-mate entitled to this respect, but it will demonstrate to the judge a modicum of teamwork.[3]

---

[3] The role of the non-speaking mooter is discussed in more detail in Ch.10.

● **Listen attentively to any feedback**

Few mooters need to be told to pay attention when the judge announces who has won the moot. But you should also listen politely to any feedback that the judge gives, even if you have lost. In fact, particularly if you have lost.

CHAPTER CHECKLIST

- Follow any dress code contained in the competition rules.
- If the competition rules are silent about dress, wear business attire or the nearest thing to it you can manage.
- Maintain your standard of dress throughout the moot.
- Use the proper forms of address when referring to judges and other mooters.
- Stand whenever the judge enters or leaves the courtroom.
- Stand whenever you address the judge or the judge addresses you directly.
- Display good manners at all times.
- Turn off your mobile phone before you enter the moot courtroom and do not turn it back on again until the moot is over.

▶ 9.21

▶ 10
Oral submissions

10.1 ▶ Prepare all you can for a moot (and you should), but winning is ultimately about your performance on the night. However thorough your research, however compelling your skeleton argument and however immaculate your dress, most moots are won and lost during the oral submissions.

This chapter is primarily concerned with the arrangement and content of oral submissions. It starts by describing the order and length of speeches at moots before examining in detail each of the constituent parts of a typical moot speech. The remainder of the chapter covers the conventions of legal speaking, time management and how to behave when others are speaking.

ORDER AND LENGTH OF SPEECHES

10.2 ▶ The order in which mooters address the court differs in English and Scottish moots. This divergence reflects the contrasting practices in the courts of the two jurisdictions. Figure 10.1 shows the usual order of speeches in England and Wales on the one hand and Scotland on the other.

As appears from figure 10.1, in England and Wales, both teams speak one after the other with leading counsel in each team speaking first and junior counsel following. The appellant then enjoys a right of reply at the end of the moot, which leading counsel normally exercises. In Scotland, by contrast, both sides' junior counsel speak before senior counsel, and it is the respondent who enjoys the last word.

10.3 ▶ **Figure 10.1:**
Usual order of speeches

Speech No.	England and Wales	Scotland
1.	Leading counsel for the appellant	Junior counsel for the appellant/reclaimer
2.	Junior counsel for the appellant	Junior counsel for the respondent
3.	Leading counsel for the respondent	Senior counsel for the appellant/reclaimer
4.	Junior counsel for the respondent	Senior counsel for the respondent
5.	Leading or junior counsel for the appellant in reply	N/A

In one important respect, the order of speeches is the same in both English and Scottish moots: it is always the appellant's team that addresses the court first (albeit leading counsel in England and Wales and junior counsel in Scotland). This order reflects the fact that in both jurisdictions it is the appellant rather than the respondent who comes to the court seeking a remedy.

The competition rules will stipulate how much speaking time each mooter is allowed. Typically it is about 10–15 minutes. Leading counsel are sometimes given more "air time" than junior counsel. In English moots, reply submissions on behalf of the appellant are usually limited to no more than five minutes.

ARRANGEMENT OF ORAL SUBMISSIONS

The Ancient Greek philosopher Plato believed that every speech should have a beginning, a middle and an end. Typical moot speeches are no different. The beginning of a moot speech consists of an introduction, the primary purpose of which is to set the scene for the remainder of the speech. Introductions to moot speeches are largely formulaic. But, by following the formula, you will achieve the primary purpose and establish some credibility with the judge. ▶ 10.4

The middle of a moot speech contains the mooter's arguments, usually a mixture of the mooter's positive and negative cases. The balance you strike between your positive and negative cases largely depends on where you appear in the order of speeches. In English moots, the appellant's counsel should use the vast majority of their main speeches (i.e., speeches 1 and 2 in figure 10.1) to develop their positive case. They will not have heard what the respondent's counsel have to say at that stage and should be wary of anticipating the detail of the respondent's arguments. The bulk of the appellant's refutation should appear in the reply submissions (speech 5), after the respondent's counsel have spoken. Conversely, leading and junior counsel for the respondent will have heard the entirety of the appellant's positive case when they get to their feet. They should both therefore include an element of refutation in their speeches.

In Scottish moots, the dynamic is different because each side speaks alternately. Save for junior counsel for the appellant/reclaimer, who speaks first, each mooter hears at least part of the other side's case before beginning his or her submissions. It is incumbent on all the subsequent speakers to respond to what has gone before. The later you appear in the speaking order, the more of the debate you will have heard and the more the judge will expect you to react to it in your speech.

The end of a moot speech consists of a conclusion that summarises the mooter's arguments and signals to the judge that the speech is drawing to a close. Conclusions should be short and use some standard phraseology.

The content of each of these three sections of a typical moot speech—the introduction, the arguments and the conclusion—is considered in detail in the next few pages. The focus is on the principal speeches that mooters make (i.e., speeches 1–4 in figure 10.1). There follows a short description of the content of reply submissions (i.e., speech 5 in figure 10.1).

INTRODUCTION

10.5 ▶ The length and content of the introduction depend on the mooter's place in the order of speeches. By far the greatest burden falls on the first mooter to address the court (*i.e.*, leading counsel for the appellant in an English moot and junior counsel for the appellant/reclaimer in a Scottish moot). The manner in which the first speaker should open his or her oral submissions is considered next. The introductions of the subsequent speakers are examined thereafter.

First speaker (for the appellant)

10.6 ▶ The first speaker's introduction should serve five principal functions: introduce the mooters from both teams; identify the subject of the moot; summarise the factual background; set an agenda for the submissions of the appellant's counsel; and ensure that the judge has received any skeleton argument or bundle of authorities prepared by the appellant's team. Each of these functions is considered below.

Introduce the mooters

10.7 ▶ The first speaker should start by introducing all of the mooters. Leading counsel for the appellant in *Cecil v Dickens*[1] might therefore begin his speech in the following way:

> "*May it please Your Lordship.*[2] *I am CJ Stryver. Together with my learned friend, Sydney Carton, I appear on behalf of the appellant in this matter, Mr Charles Dickens. The respondent, Mr Henry Cecil, is represented by my learned friends Sally Mannering and Roger Thursby.*"

There are three short points to note about these opening words:

- The phrase "May it please Your Lordship", while rather formal, is widely used for starting speeches, both by mooters and practitioners. A less grandiose option is to say simply, "My Lord, . . ."
- Do not give your name if it is clear that the judge already knows who you are, for example if he or she calls on you by name to begin your oral submissions.
- As you introduce your fellow mooters to the judge, glance briefly towards each of them in turn. These gestures will ensure that the judge knows who is who.

Identify the subject of the moot

10.8 ▶ Having introduced the mooters, the first speaker should next identify the subject of the moot. Given that the judge will almost certainly have read the moot problem already, a short summary normally suffices. In *Cecil v Dickens*, for example, leading counsel for the appellant might say as follows:

> "*This is the hearing of the appeal against the decision of Mr Justice Steerforth sitting in the Queen's Bench Division. The learned judge held that Mr Dickens gave*

---

[1] Leading counsel for the appellant is the first speaker because *Cecil v Dickens* is an English moot.
[2] You would, of course, substitute here the words "Your Ladyship", "Your Ladyships" or "Your Lordships" as appropriate depending on the make-up of your moot tribunal. The same point applies to all of the examples in this chapter and Ch.11.

negligent advice to Mr Cecil about a potential claim by Mr Cecil against a firm of accountants called Wickfield's."

Summarise the facts

Even though the judge should be well aware of the facts of the moot problem, some mooting competitions adhere to the convention that the first speaker must formally offer a summary of the facts. You can make this offer with the words, "Would Your Lordship like to be reminded of the facts of this case?" If you ask this question and the judge's response is affirmative, keep your summary short and do not proceed to read out large chunks of the moot problem verbatim. Focus instead on the broad subject matter of the claim and the stage that the proceedings have reached. In *Cecil v Dickens*, for instance, the appellant's leading counsel might summarise the facts in the following way:

▶ 10.9

> *"In these proceedings, Mr Cecil alleges that Mr Dickens gave him negligent advice during a conversation in a pub in early 2010. Mr Cecil complains, in particular, that Mr Dickens failed to mention that a limitation period applied to the potential claim against Mr Cecil's accountants. Mr Cecil waited for more than three years before trying to bring his claim, by which time the relevant limitation period had expired. At trial, Mr Justice Steerforth ordered Mr Dickens to pay Mr Cecil the sum of £100,000. That sum represented the value that the learned judge ascribed to Mr Cecil's potential claim against the accountants."*

When providing a summary of the facts, you can legitimately highlight those facts that help your case (just as you can in the introduction to any skeleton argument you draft)[3] as long as your description is accurate. The example above is pretty balanced, but it does still draw attention to the facts that Mr Dickens's advice was given in a pub and that it took Mr Cecil three years to try to bring his claim against the accountants. Both of these facts assist Mr Dickens.

Set an agenda

The next task of the first speaker is to set an agenda by outlining the division of labour between the members of the appellant's team. Each member of a moot team usually deals with a different ground of appeal. The appellant's leading counsel in *Cecil v Dickens* might therefore set the agenda in the following way:

▶ 10.10

> *"Mr Dickens appeals against the decision of the learned judge on two grounds. The first is that Mr Dickens owed no duty of care to Mr Cecil. I intend to address Your Lordship on this ground of appeal. The second is that, even if a duty of care was owed to Mr Cecil, Mr Dickens did not breach it. My learned friend Mr Carton will address Your Lordship on that ground of appeal."*

Check the judge has received your skeleton argument and bundle of authorities

If the teams have prepared skeleton arguments or bundles of authorities, the first speaker's final task is to ensure that the judge has received the documents that the appellant's team has

▶ 10.11

---

[3] This aspect of drafting skeleton arguments is considered in Ch.4.

produced. If you are speaking first and you notice that the judge already has your skeleton and bundle, skip this task. But if you are not sure, double-check, for example by asking as follows:

> *"Before I move on to the first of my submissions, may I confirm that Your Lordship has received a copy of the appellant's skeleton argument and its bundle of authorities?"*

If, by some misfortune, the judge answers "no" to this question, you can hand up the spare copy that you prepared and brought with you to the moot in dutiful observance of the advice contained in Ch.8.

Illustration

10.12 ▶ For ease of reference, figure 10.2 draws together the various elements of the first speaker's introduction described above. It assumes that the first speaker does not offer the judge a summary of the facts of the moot problem.

10.13 ▶ **Figure 10.2:**
Introduction of the first speaker

May it please Your Lordship. I am CJ Stryver. Together with my learned friend, Sydney Carton, I appear on behalf of the appellant in this matter, Mr Charles Dickens. The respondent, Mr Henry Cecil, is represented by my learned friends Sally Mannering and Roger Thursby.

This is the hearing of the appeal against the decision of Mr Justice Steerforth sitting in the Queen's Bench Division. The learned judge held that Mr Dickens gave negligent advice to Mr Cecil about a potential claim by Mr Cecil against a firm of accountants called Wickfield's.

Mr Dickens appeals against the decision of the learned judge on two grounds. The first is that Mr Dickens owed no duty of care to Mr Cecil. I intend to address Your Lordship on this ground of appeal. The second is that, even if a duty of care was owed to Mr Cecil, Mr Dickens did not breach it. My learned friend Mr Carton will address Your Lordship on that ground of appeal.

Before I move on to the first of my submissions, may I confirm that Your Lordship has received a copy of the appellant's skeleton argument and its bundle of authorities?

Subsequent speakers

10.14 ▶ In comparison with the first speaker, subsequent speakers have relatively little to say by way of introduction. In particular, there is no need for them to identify the subject of the moot or offer a summary of the facts. What each subsequent speaker does say depends to a large extent on where he or she appears in the order of speeches.

First speaker for the respondent

10.15 ▶ As figure 10.1 shows, the first speaker for the respondent in an English moot is leading counsel, who appears third in the order of speeches. In Scottish moots, the first speaker for the respondent is junior counsel, who appears second.

The introduction of the first mooter for the respondent should identify the members of the respondent's team and provide a short agenda for the respondent's submissions. In all likelihood, that agenda will mirror the division of labour between the appellant's counsel. For example, leading counsel for the respondent in *Cecil v Dickens* might begin her submissions in the following way:

> *"May it please Your Lordship. My name is Sally Mannering. Together with my learned junior, Mr Thursby, I represent the respondent, Mr Cecil. My learned junior and I have divided our submissions in the same way as my learned friends opposite. I will therefore address Your Lordship on the first ground of appeal, namely whether a duty of care arises in negligence. Mr Thursby will then deal with the second ground of appeal—whether there has been a breach of that duty."*

If the parties have prepared skeleton arguments or bundles of authorities, the first speaker for the respondent should also check that the judge has received the respondent's documents and hand up a copy if necessary.

Second speakers for both teams

The introductions of the second speakers for both teams should set the agenda for their own submissions by reference to the arguments already advanced by their team-mates. In *Cecil v Dickens*, for example, junior counsel for the appellant might open his submissions in this way:

▶ 10.16

> *"May it please Your Lordship. I am Sydney Carton, junior counsel for Mr Dickens. My learned leader has already addressed Your Lordship on Mr Dickens's first ground of appeal. I will now address Your Lordship on the second ground of appeal. My submissions will therefore deal with whether Mr Dickens breached any duty of care that Your Lordship finds he owed to Mr Cecil."*

ARGUMENTS

With the introduction safely negotiated, you can proceed to the longest and most important part of your moot speech, the arguments. In this section of your oral submissions, you develop the arguments that comprise your positive and negative cases.

▶ 10.17

There is no one-size-fits-all formula for presenting arguments. In general terms, you must convey to the judge the reasoning that underpins each of your points. As Ch.3 explained, persuasive legal arguments are founded on valid deductive and inductive reasoning. Each of your arguments will usually therefore involve either the application of a valid general rule to the facts of the moot problem (a deductive argument) or the comparison of one or more authorities with the facts of the moot problem (an inductive argument).

Whatever type of arguments you make, you must find a persuasive way to communicate them to the judge. The key is to express your points clearly. More easily said than done, admittedly, but the guidelines offered in the next few pages should help.

Arrange your arguments effectively

10.18 ▷ The order in which you present your arguments can affect their persuasiveness. Say—as is usually the case—you have several arguments, some of which are stronger than others. How should you arrange them so as to maximise the impact of your strongest points?

The latest thinking, which is backed by psychological studies, is that audiences tend to remember best what they hear at the start of a speech (the "primacy effect") and at the end (the "recency effect"). All other things being equal, you should therefore lead off with your strongest point. The judge will be "all ears" at the beginning of your oral submissions and a convincing argument at that stage should hit home. But finish your speech strongly too, whether by presenting a powerful argument that you have kept in reserve or by reiterating your best point in summary form. Your last argument will reverberate in the judge's mind after you sit down, just when the judge is making notes about your performance.

Consider too the order of your positive and negative cases. As a general rule, it is best to make the former before the latter. You want to define the debate in your own terms and it is usually easier to do so if you present your positive case first. The points you make in refutation can be addressed in a group at the end of your oral submissions. But do not regard this arrangement as inflexible. It can be extremely effective to precede your positive case with a point of refutation. This approach works best if it is confined to a single, telling point on an important issue that you can deliver swiftly. If you find yourself in that position, you might launch your attack in this way: "My Lord, before I turn to my first submission, I would like briefly to address an important point that my learned friends opposite made earlier. . . ." You must then avoid becoming bogged down in the detail of your opponents' argument. Make your point quickly, show how it undermines your opponents' argument and then move on to your positive case.

Start each positive argument with a summary

10.19 ▷ Every time you make an argument as part of your positive case, begin with a short summary of it, ideally, just one or two sentences. You will give the judge an immediate sense of where you are going and provide an anchor to which he or she can attach the detail of your argument. For example, leading counsel for the appellant in *Cecil v Dickens*, having completed the introduction in figure 10.2, might proceed as follows:

> *"I now turn to my submissions. My Lord, Mr Dickens submits that he owed no duty of care to Mr Cecil because the current test for determining the existence of duties of care in negligence to avoid pure economic loss is not satisfied in this case."*

This sort of summary leads readily into the meat of the argument, namely what the current test is (the major premise of the underlying syllogism) and why it is not satisfied in this case (the minor premise). Such a summary may prompt an interventionist judge to jump in immediately with a question designed to focus your argument on a particular issue. So much the better. You will then have a good idea of the judge's main concern and can adjust your submissions on the point accordingly.

Refer to authorities systematically

Much of the argument section of your oral submissions will involve walking the judge through the authorities on which you rely. Whenever you take the judge to one of your authorities, you must explain what you are doing and why. If the judge does not appreciate the principle that you are drawing from an authority, your argument will be significantly undermined.

▶ 10.20

A seven-step guide

Whenever you take the judge to a new authority as you develop an argument, follow the seven steps outlined below:

▶ 10.21

● **Step 1: explain the relevance of the authority**

Before you ask the judge to read an authority, explain why you say it is relevant. Say, for example, that you are referring to a reported case that you assert contains a relevant legal test. You might introduce it as follows:

> "My Lord, I turn now to the test that applies in cases of this type. In my submission, the relevant test is set out in the recent case of . . ."

● **Step 2: cite the authority**

If neither team has previously referred to the authority at the moot, provide a full and correct citation. The written and oral forms of citations differ. You cannot therefore simply read out verbatim the written version. Table 10.3 provides three examples of the written and oral versions of the same citations. Note, in particular, that in case report citations the letter "v" is always pronounced "and" or "against" rather than "vee" or "versus", and that the letter "R" is always pronounced "the Crown" rather than "are".

Table 10.3:
Written and oral forms of citations

▶ 10.22

Written citation	Oral citation
Customs and Excise Commissioners v Barclays Bank plc [2007] 1 AC 181	"Customs and Excise Commissioners against Barclays Bank plc, which is reported in volume one of the *Appeal Cases* reports for 2007 at page one hundred and eighty-one."
R v Jackson [1999] 1 All ER 572	"The Crown against Jackson, reported in the first volume of the *All England Law Reports* for 1999 at page five hundred and seventy-two."
Jackson & Powell on Professional Liability, 7th ed (2013)	"Jackson and Powell on Professional Liability, seventh edition, which was published in 2013."

● **Step 3: ensure the judge has a copy**

Once you have cited the authority, make sure that the judge has a copy of it. If you are providing your authorities to the judge one by one, this is the juncture at which you should hand up a copy (via the moot court clerk if there is one). If you have served a bundle of authorities in advance of the moot, identify the tab or page number at which the authority appears in the bundle.

● Step 4: offer a summary of the facts if the authority is a case

When you refer to a reported decision that has not previously been cited at the moot, offer to provide the judge with a summary of the facts. You might do so by asking, "Is Your Lordship familiar with the facts of this case?" or "Would Your Lordship like to be reminded of the facts of this case?" The judge may decline your offer if he or she has read the decision or time is short. There will be occasions, however, when the judge indicates that a reminder of the salient facts would assist. You should then provide a summary.[4]

● Step 5: identify the relevant passage of the authority

Identify the passage of the authority that you want the judge to read. Do so carefully and slowly. Many a mooter has left a judge floundering by trotting out a page number and then launching immediately into a quotation. There are various ways of identifying relevant passages. You might say, "May I refer Your Lordship to the judgment of Lord [??] at paragraph [??] of the report?" or "Would Your Lordship please turn to page [??] of the report? The relevant passage starts about two-thirds of the way down the page with the words [??]." Having precisely identified the relevant passage, make sure that the judge has found it before you take the next step. If the judge is still flicking through the case report, wait a moment or two until he or she is ready. Repeat the reference if necessary.

● Step 6: read the key passage of the authority

If the passage on which you rely is no more than about seven or eight lines long, read it out loud when, but only when, you are certain that the judge is looking at it. You can then place emphasis on the words you regard as important. If the passage is longer, invite the judge to read it and remain silent while he or she does so.

● Step 7: apply the authority to the facts

Once the judge has heard or read the passage of the authority on which you rely, apply it to the facts of the moot problem. Start this process by distilling the passage into a pithy legal principle. You might, for example, say that, "In short, My Lord, the court in that case said that . . ." or "It is apparent from this judgment that the proper test in cases of this type is . . ." Having stated the principle, apply it to the facts of the moot problem. Make specific reference to particular facts. If, for example, the principle you derive from the authority is that the court must consider all of the relevant facts, tell the judge which facts are relevant and why.

Illustration

10.23 ▶ Figure 10.4 contains an example oral submission based on the possible line of argument for the appellant in *Cecil v Dickens* summarised in figure 3.4 in Ch.3. The submission includes each of the seven steps outlined above. In the interests of clarity, figure 10.4 is an abbreviated

---

4 As explained in Ch.5, the notes you prepare for the moot should include summaries of the facts of each reported case on which you rely. You can refer to these notes at this point in your oral submissions.

Figure 10.4:
Oral submission referring to an authority

My Lord, I now turn to the test that applies to determine the existence of duties of care in negligence to avoid pure economic loss. In my submission, the proper test is the so-called "multi-test" approach. This test was applied by the House of Lords in Customs and Excise Commissioners against Barclays Bank plc, which is reported in volume one of the *Appeal Cases* reports for 2007 at page one hundred and eighty-one.
[At this point, you would hand up a copy of the authority to the judge or identify the relevant tab or page number of your bundle of authorities.]
Is Your Lordship familiar with the facts of this case?
[If the judge answered "no", you would provide a summary.]
Would Your Lordship please turn to paragraph eighty-two of the report, which is at page two hundred and thirteen?
[You would then wait until you were certain that the judge had found this reference.]
Paragraph eighty-two is part of the judgment of Lord Mance. The passage on which I rely starts at the beginning of the paragraph. It reads as follows:

> *"The conceptual basis on which courts decide whether a duty of care exists in particular circumstances has been repeatedly examined. Three broad approaches have been suggested, involving consideration of (a) whether there has been an assumption of responsibility, (b) whether a three-fold test of foreseeability, proximity and "fairness, justice and reasonableness" has been satisfied or (c) whether the alleged duty would be "incremental" to previous cases."*

My Lord, in this passage, Lord Mance identifies three approaches. He goes on to apply each of them in turn.
[You might next take the judge to each passage in which Lord Mance applied these tests.]
In my submission, the proper approach in this case is to follow the approach of Lord Mance in Customs and Excise Commissioners against Barclays, and to apply each of the three tests he identified to the facts of the moot problem. The first test is whether there has been an assumption of responsibility. Would Your Lordship please now look at the moot problem?
[You would wait until you were certain that the judge was looking at the moot problem.]
Your Lordship will see that, during the contentious conversation between the parties in January 2010, Mr Dickens told Mr Cecil that, "If you decide to take matters forward, you should consult a law firm called Barkis & Traddles, which specialises in litigation." In my submission, these words made it clear to Mr Cecil that Mr Dickens was not assuming responsibility towards him. In fact, Mr Dickens was expressly disavowing responsibility. He told Mr Cecil that he should consult another solicitor if he wanted to proceed with his claim against Wickfield's. In those circumstances, it is submitted that Mr Cecil cannot satisfy the first limb of the multi-test approach.
[You would then proceed to make submissions on each of the remaining tests identified by Lord Mance.]

version of what you might actually say in practice and includes several explanatory notes in bold and square brackets.

Refer periodically to your skeleton argument

10.25 ▶ If you serve a skeleton argument, refer to it in your oral submissions. The judge will have read your skeleton and will expect you to develop the arguments contained in it. If you fail to tie your speech to your skeleton, you risk confusing the judge about what your case really is.

You can achieve this linkage by referring directly to your skeleton argument from time to time during your speech. Counsel for the appellant might, for example, say this at an appropriate moment: "As Your Lordship will have seen from paragraph [??] of our skeleton argument, the appellant relies in support of this submission on the case of . . ." The references you make to your skeleton argument should be brief. Do not read out large chunks word for word or the judge will quickly become bored.

Know when to stop

10.26 ▶ As you develop your arguments, try to gauge how the judge is reacting to them. A quizzical look, a shake of the head or an unhelpful question probably indicates that the judge is not with you on a particular point. If so, try to get the judge back on board as quickly as possible. But if you have already made a submission as persuasively as you can, do not repeat it several times using slightly different language in the hope that the judge will change his or her mind. Move on to your next point.

CONCLUSION

10.27 ▶ Compared to advocates in professional practice, mooters have very little speaking time at their disposal. You will not therefore be expected to conclude your oral submissions with a comprehensive summary of what you said only a few minutes previously. You should nonetheless round off your speech with a few up-beat sentences that summarise your case. You should also tell the judge exactly what remedy you are seeking.

Make sure that the judge realises you are moving on to your conclusion. You can do so by starting your closing remarks with the words, "My Lord, in conclusion, . . ." or "My Lord, to conclude, . . ." Alternatively, you might simply pause after finishing your last argument and start your conclusion with the words, "My Lord, . . ."

Always end your oral submissions with the words, "Unless I can be of any further assistance to Your Lordship, those are my submissions." This formula, which is used in professional practice as well as mooting, indicates that you have reached the end of your speech and gives the judge a chance to ask any final questions. Nine times out of ten, the judge will not take up your invitation and you will be free to sit down.

Figure 10.5 contains an example of how junior counsel for the appellant (i.e., the second speaker) in the illustrative case of *Cecil v Dickens* might round off his oral submissions.

▶ 10.28

Figure 10.5:
Conclusion

My Lord, as my learned friend Mr Stryver explained during his speech, this case does not satisfy the test that the English courts now apply to determine whether a duty of care arises in negligence to avoid pure economic loss. Even if, contrary to that submission, Your Lordship finds that Mr Dickens did owe a duty of care to Mr Cecil, Mr Dickens did not breach that duty for the reasons I have outlined in my speech. It is therefore submitted that this appeal should be allowed. Unless I can be of any further assistance to Your Lordship, those are my submissions.

REPLY SUBMISSIONS

▶ 10.29

Just like other moot speeches, the appellant's submissions in reply should have a beginning, a middle and an end, but both the beginning and the end can be very short indeed. The focus of this speech is the middle, the handful (or fewer) of points that you make to refute your opponent's arguments.

Keep the introduction to your reply submissions to a minimum. You might even say as little as this: "May it please Your Lordship. I have [three] points in reply. The first concerns, . . . My second point relates to . . . My final point is . . ." It is normally sensible to preface each of your points of refutation with a quick *précis* of the arguments of your opponents to which you are responding.

When you have finished all of your points in reply, conclude with the standard words, "Unless I can be of any further assistance to Your Lordship, those are my reply submissions." Few judges ask questions at this point. The oral submissions are over and judges are normally turning their minds to their next task—deciding who should win the moot.

LEGAL SPEAKING CONVENTIONS

▶ 10.30

Just as lawyers observe certain conventions when they write,[5] so they follow certain informal "rules" when they speak. Some of these legal speaking conventions help to maintain the requisite atmosphere of formality and civility in the courtroom. Others help the judge to follow the advocates' submissions. A selection of the most important speaking conventions for mooting purposes is described below.

Avoid speaking in the first person

▶ 10.31

As Ch.4 explained, mooters should not express personal opinions in their skeleton arguments. The same rule applies when they make submissions orally. Except in very rare circumstances, shun phrases like, "In my/our opinion, . . .", "It seems to me/us that . . ." and "I/We think that . . ." Use the following impersonal expressions instead: "In my/our submission, . . .", "It is submitted that . . ." and "The appellant/respondent submits that . . ."

---

[5] Ch.4 discusses legal writing conventions.

Provide regular "signposts"

10.32 ▶ Throughout your oral submissions, give the judge periodic indications of where your argument is heading. Without these "signposts", your submissions may lack coherence and be difficult to follow. "Signposts" can take any of the following forms:

● **Lists**

One of the most effective ways of keeping the judge clear about the direction and structure of your submissions is to make regular use of lists: explain that you have a certain number of points to make on a particular issue and then go through them consecutively. For example, towards the beginning of your speech, you might say this: "My Lord, in support of the first ground of appeal, I have three submissions. They are, first, that . . . , second, that . . . and, third, that . . . . Turning to my first submission, . . ." When judges hear you say that you have a list of points, they will often pick up their pens to make notes. Follow the judge's pen when you speak to ensure that he or she has jotted down all the points on your list.

● **Connecting phrases**

You will often want to make connections between your various points and must ensure that the judge understands the links you are attempting to establish. You might, for instance, identify a rule of law and then refer the judge to an authority from which you contend that it derives. Having stated the rule, you might say as follows: "In support of this submission, I rely on the case of . . ." or "In my submission, this principle can be derived from the case of . . ." Other connecting phrases include "in addition", "on the one hand . . . on the other . . ." and "in summary".

● **Separating phrases**

Just as important as linking your submissions together is distinguishing between the different points that you make. There are various ways of signalling to the judge that you are moving from one point to the next. They include, "My Lord, I now turn to consider . . ." and "My Lord, my next point/submission is . . ."

Do not be afraid of appearing overly simplistic when you use "signposts". The judge will not be as familiar as you are with the material and will probably be delighted to receive a few "steers".

Express thanks for any assistance

10.33 ▶ In the course of your speech, the judge, your mooting partner or your opponents may attempt to assist you in some way. The judge might, for example, indicate that he or she has already read an authority to which you intend to refer, thereby avoiding the need for you to summarise its facts. Alternatively, your team-mate or one of your opponents might correct an inaccurate case citation that you have just provided. Even if the intervention is not that helpful, you should express thanks in one of the following ways:

- *"I am grateful"*
- *"I am grateful to Your Lordship/Your Ladyship/my learned friend"*
- *"I am obliged"*
- *"I am obliged to Your Lordship/Your Ladyship/my learned friend"*

A word of warning, however. Thanking the judge should not descend into obsequious-ness. If the judge makes a helpful intervention, perhaps by suggesting an argument in your favour that you had not thought of, stick to one of the phrases identified above and avoid any temptation to gush that the judge is "SO right".

Disagree with the judge politely

▌10.34

Conversely, you may have occasion during your oral submissions to correct or disagree with something the judge has said. Do so politely. You can show the requisite deference by offering your counter-view tentatively, even if you know you are right. If the judge has referred to the wrong page of a case report, for example, you might say, "My Lord, I think I am right in saying that the case report begins at page 150, not page 50." (This situation is one of those rare instances when you can properly speak in the first person.)

If you disagree with the judge on a more fundamental issue, such as the principle to be drawn from a particular authority, you may begin your response using the words "with respect" or "in my respectful submission". These phrases are perfectly appropriate if spoken with genuine intent. But if there is the faintest hint of sarcasm or annoyance in your voice, you will sound as though you actually have no respect for the judge at all. The danger is even more acute if you use the phrase "with the greatest of respect". It is therefore best avoided.

Be wary of using humour

▌10.35

Prepared "gags" almost always founder in moot speeches. However funny you might find them before the moot, they will probably induce pin-drop silence or embarrassed titters when you deliver them. As the classical rhetorician Quintilian put it nearly 2,000 years ago, "there are no jests so insipid as those which parade the fact that they are intended to be witty".[6]

Humour does have a place in the moot courtroom, however. An amusing remark made on the spur of the moment will add colour to your presentation and demonstrate intelligence and self-confidence. Humour need not be downright funny to be effective. A clever turn of phrase or a lightness of touch in your vocabulary—an unusual or vivid word—can bring a smile to the judge's face and improve your chances of winning the moot.

Avoid inflammatory remarks

▌10.36

Judges are not impressed by heated language, whether they read it in a skeleton argument or hear it in oral submissions. Take particular care when delivering your speech not to make per-sonal attacks on your opponents, even if they have made snide remarks about you or your team-mate. So-called *ad hominem* argument usually does far more damage to the speaker than to the victim. Rise above it.

TIME MANAGEMENT

▌10.37

Whatever period of time the competition rules allow for you to speak, make the most of it and do not overrun. Many mooters get into difficulties with timing. Some are overly ambitious about how much they can fit in, then panic when they discover that their time is up and rush

---

6   Quintilian, *Institutio Oratoria*, VI, 3, 26.

what remains of their submissions. Others underestimate how quickly they will complete their submissions and are forced to sit down with valuable speaking time unutilised.

The first step in managing your time properly is to know before the moot how long your prepared submissions should last. Timing should therefore be part of every mooter's practice regimen.[7] But you can never know in advance precisely how long your submissions will take at the moot, particularly if your allotted time includes interventions from the bench. You therefore need to build flexibility into your speech.

In order to avoid running drastically over your allotted time, prepare in advance a conclusion of a specific length. In most moots, you will receive some warning (usually from the moot court clerk) as you approach the end of your speaking time. If you know that you will be given a 30-second warning, for example, prepare a conclusion that lasts for about 30 seconds.[8] Wherever you are in your speech when you receive the warning, you can quickly complete the point you are making and skip to the start of your conclusion. If you will not receive a warning, you can prepare a shorter conclusion of perhaps 15 seconds. If your time expires before you complete your submissions, you can then jump to your conclusion in the knowledge that you will exceed your allotted time only marginally.

You can plan for finishing more quickly than you anticipate by having additional material up your sleeve. You might, for example, prepare short and long versions of your final argument. You can resort to the latter if you realise that you have time to spare. You might even prepare a short supplemental argument if you can think of a point that is not a mere makeweight.

NON-SPEAKERS

10.38 ▶ You can have a significant impact on the oral submissions even when you are not speaking. A display of bad manners can damage your prospects of success, for example, as Ch. 9 explains. But non-speaking mooters can make a positive contribution too. Their role differs according to whether the speaker is the mooter's team-mate or an opponent.

Team-mate speaking
10.39 ▶ In this situation, your principal task is to provide whatever help you can to your team-mate without drawing attention to yourself. The assistance you render might include the following:

● **Helping with judicial interventions**
You can probably be of most assistance if your team-mate is struggling to answer a question from the judge. If you have a satisfactory response, communicate it to your team-mate either by scribbling it down on a piece of paper or a "post-it" note or, if the judge gives permission, by speaking to your team-mate quickly and quietly. Never attempt to address the judge directly unless he or she invites you to do so.

---

[7]   Ch.7 considers in detail how to practise oral submissions.
[8]   By way of example, the conclusion set out in figure 10.5 should take around 30 seconds to deliver.

● **Helping with references to documents**
If your team-mate has given the judge an incorrect page reference to an authority or is unable to recall a reference with sufficient speed, you can be poised with the correct information.

● **Helping with pace**
If your team-mate is talking too quickly, you can signal to slow down, perhaps with an inconspicuous hand gesture. Likewise, if you notice that the judge is losing interest in a particular submission, you can usher your team-mate on to the next point.

In order to provide assistance of this type, you have to follow with some care not only your team-mate's submissions and the documents to which he or she is referring, but also the judge's reaction. You must therefore concentrate on what is going on, even if you have just finished your own speech and feel like kicking back and relaxing.

Opponent speaking

Your primary objective when an opponent is speaking is to make a decent note of any points to which you or your team-mate should respond during your speeches. If you have prepared thoroughly for the moot, you will already have a good idea of what the other side will say. But your opponents will inevitably make submissions during their speeches that you have not pre-empted.

▷ 10.40

Your note must be sufficiently detailed to convey the gist of your point and provide an adequate prompt when you make your submission in reply. You will develop your own methodology of note-taking, but the following tips might help:

● **Keep the note short**
You will not have much time in which to write your note and even less time in which to read it during your speech. So keep it brief.

● **Make a note of your opponent's actual words**
When you jot down the gist of an opponent's submission, it usually helps to record the key words or phrases that he or she actually uses. You will summarise the submission more accurately that way and the judge is more likely to recall it when you make your argument in reply.

● **Separate your opponent's submission from your response**
In your note, clearly delineate what your opponent said from the point you intend to make in response. At a minimum, these two elements of your note should begin on separate lines. You might even consider using differently coloured pens.

CHAPTER CHECKLIST

- Find out in advance of the moot where you will appear in the order of speeches and how much speaking time you will have at your disposal.

▷ 10.41

- Open your speech by making the appropriate introductions and setting an agenda.

- Present your arguments persuasively by:
  - Arranging them effectively.
  - Starting each argument with a short summary of it.
  - Referring to each authority on which you rely using the seven-step guide outlined in this chapter.
  - Linking your arguments to your skeleton argument.
- Conclude your speech with a short summary of your case and a request for the relief you seek.
- Observe the conventions of legal speaking throughout your oral submissions.
- Keep to the speaking time allocated to you by using the techniques described in this chapter.
- Concentrate and be productive while others are speaking.

11

Judicial interventions

Unless you appear before an unusually docile moot judge, your oral submissions will be punctu- ▶ 11.1
ated by one or more interventions from the bench. Many mooters contemplate the prospect of
judicial interventions with morbid dread. The purpose of this chapter is to shed some light on
this murky subject and, in the process, to dispel some of the fear associated with it. The chapter
begins with a quick look at what judicial interventions are, before considering the key to answering them effectively: thorough preparation. The chapter then provides a suggested approach to
answering judicial interventions and a list of sample questions before concluding with advice on
how to cope with the most feared beast of the mooting deep—the question you cannot answer.

WHAT IS A JUDICIAL INTERVENTION?

A judicial intervention is a question asked by the moot judge. You should expect the judge to ▶ 11.2
interrupt you with questions several times during your oral submissions. The judge may also
ask you questions after you complete your prepared submissions, but before you sit down.
Most judges try to ensure that they subject each mooter to a similar level of questioning.

The power of judges to ask questions is an important feature of mooting. It enables
judges to test the mooters' familiarity with the material, their ability to think on their feet and
their overall skills as advocates. The manner in which mooters respond to judicial interventions
is often decisive in determining who wins moots. Those mooters who provide the more cogent
and articulate responses to the judge's questions often prevail even if their prepared submissions are not as impressive as those of their opponents. Judicial interventions consequently
present you with a wonderful opportunity to influence the judge. Welcome them.

PREPARATION, PREPARATION, PREPARATION

The key to dealing effectively with judicial interventions is preparation. If you prepare properly ▶ 11.3
for the moot, you will cope with just about anything the judge throws at you. If the judge
requests information or clarification, the relevant knowledge should be at your fingertips. If the
judge challenges one of your arguments, you should be able to fashion a suitable riposte. If the
judge's question is irrelevant, you should recognise it as such and deal with it accordingly. As
your experience as a mooter grows, you should find that the moots in which you perform best
are those in which the judge asks you the most penetrating questions; they are the questions
that allow you to display the full extent of your knowledge and skills.

The critical role of preparation in answering questions from the bench doubtless explains why advanced advocacy textbooks tend not to discuss judicial interventions as a distinct topic. They evidently assume that the advocate with full command of his or her brief will deal effectively with any sensible question the judge might ask. While this assumption is undoubtedly correct, there are nonetheless certain ways in which you can maximise your chances of cogently answering the judge's questions.

Target your preparation

11.4 ▶ Focus your preparation for judicial interventions by identifying the key issues on which the judge is likely to concentrate. The goal here is not to work out *precisely* what the judge will ask. It is rather to anticipate the likely concerns of the judge in general terms so that you can identify the material (including any notes) you will need to have readily to hand when the judge intervenes. The three steps set out below should help you to isolate the issues that will probably most interest the judge:

● **Identify weaknesses in your case**
The judge is most likely to question you about the weaker aspects of your case. Moot problems are designed so that both sides have strengths and weaknesses. Your arguments will therefore inevitably have a soft underbelly. As part of your preparation for the moot, identify the weak spots in your argument and consider how best to defend them from the kinds of questions the judge might ask.

● **Identify points of disagreement with your opponents**
Another area that judges like to probe with questions is the flashpoint of controversy between the parties. Judges want to see mooters respond directly to their opponents' case. A careful review of the other side's skeleton argument (if one is served) and list of authorities should therefore provide you with clues to the questions that the judge might ask. Look, in particular, for any authorities your opponents cite that appear to be at odds with authorities on which you rely. The judge may ask why your authority is preferable.

● **Practise in front of an audience**
As Ch.7 explained, pre-moot practice often helps to anticipate judicial interventions. For maximum benefit, practise in front of an audience. The obvious candidate is your team-mate, who can readily play the role of the judge and intervene frequently and incisively. But anyone will do. Indeed, non-lawyers sometimes ask the most revealing questions because they focus on the logic of the argument rather than on the legal niceties. If you cannot practise your submissions in this way, at least hold a brainstorming session with your mooting partner to discuss the questions that the judge might ask you both.

When you target your preparation for judicial interventions, assume that the judge will ask sensible questions. Mooters who fear that the judge might ask them *anything*, however off-beam or unreasonable, cause themselves unnecessary worry. After all, an irrelevant question can be dealt with as such.

Gather materials for possible answers

Once you have identified the issues the judge is likely to ask about, ensure that you will have readily available at the moot the material you will need to answer the judge's questions. Some information will be in your head, the product of your hard work in the build-up to the moot. But do not rely entirely on your memory. Prepare brief, user-friendly notes of answers to the questions you most expect to be asked[1] and have to hand any documents, suitably highlighted, that you may wish to address.

▶ 11.5

ANSWERING QUESTIONS

Your preparation for the moot may have been sufficiently thorough to provide you with the material you need to answer a particular question from the judge, but you might still deal with it ineffectively. If you jump in and attempt to answer the question too quickly, for example, you might miss something the judge says and provide only a partial response.

▶ 11.6

Set out below is a short list of guidelines for answering questions. Follow it each time the judge intervenes and you will not go far wrong.

● Listen carefully to the question

This is Rule Number One. If you do not listen to the question, you will not understand it. If you do not understand the question, you cannot answer it properly. If you do not answer the question properly, perhaps by giving incomplete or irrelevant information, the judge may regard you as incompetent. Listening carefully to the question means listening to all of it. So let the judge finish speaking before you commence your response.[2]

● Ask the judge to repeat the question if necessary

Even if you listen carefully to the question, you may not follow precisely what the judge said. Do not be embarrassed to ask the judge to repeat the question. On the contrary, it is imperative that you do so. You might simply say as follows: "Would Your Lordship please repeat/rephrase the question?" Another, slightly lengthier, option is to say, "I am afraid that I did not entirely follow Your Lordship's question. Would Your Lordship please repeat it?" If you still do not understand the question, reformulate it in your own words and ask the judge to confirm that your understanding is correct.

● Give the judge a response there and then

Always provide an immediate answer to the judge's question. Mooters often reply to judicial interventions by saying, "I will deal with Your Lordship's question later in my submissions." This approach is a mistake. It suggests evasiveness. Address the point straight away, if only briefly. You may intend to deal with the issue in detail later in your submissions. If so, still give an immediate response, but preface it by saying words to the following effect: "My Lord, I intend to address this point in detail later in my submissions. In short, the answer is . . .". If it makes sense to do so, bring forward the submission that you were going to make and incorporate it

---

1   Ch. 5 discusses in detail how to prepare notes for judicial interventions.
2   As Ch.9 explained, interrupting the judge is also a breach of mooting etiquette.

into your reply to the question. You will then demonstrate admirable flexibility and a command of the subject matter.

● Watch out for the waffle

Verbosity can easily strike mooters who are drawn away from their prepared material by a question from the judge. To avoid this pitfall, answer every question as succinctly and directly as you can. If you feel that your answer is wandering from the point, bring it swiftly to a close.

● Never forget the basics of speaking in court

Some mooters let their guards down when they enter the "broken play" of responding to judicial interventions. Make sure that you continue to concentrate on the basics of courtroom advocacy: do not speak too quickly; do not gesticulate wildly; and keep your eyes on the judge. You may even find that your advocacy becomes less forced, more fluid and consequently more persuasive when you respond to judicial interventions.

SAMPLE QUESTIONS

11.7 ▶ Some questions come up regularly at moots, whatever the subject matter of the moot problem. They tend to fall into one of four categories, each of which is described below. Within each category, a selection of "stock" questions is also provided with some suggestions for answering them. When you prepare for moots, make sure you can answer these sorts of questions.

Questions seeking information

11.8 ▶ Sometimes, judges just want information from you, be it about the moot problem, an authority you rely on or something you have said. The following are examples of this type of question:

● "I'm sorry. I didn't hear what you said" or "Can you please repeat your last point?"

If the judge asks a question like this, the chances are that your voice did not carry to the bench or the judge "tuned out" for a moment when you were speaking. There is no need to craft a clever answer to this type of question. Just repeat what you said and stay cool. Nerves can make you babble even when faced with the simplest inquiry.

● "What persuasive force should I attribute to this authority?" or "Does this authority bind me?"

Many judges ask one or other of these questions as a matter of course when mooters cite an authority from a foreign jurisdiction or rely on a decision of a court that is lower than the moot court in the court hierarchy. If you are to answer these questions effectively, you must be familiar with the doctrine of precedent and how it applies to the authorities on which you rely.[3]

---

[3] Ch.3 explains the court hierarchies in the United Kingdom and discusses the extent to which decisions of one court bind others.

● **"Has this case been considered in any subsequent decision?"**
In order to elicit this type of question, you may have referred the judge to a helpful passage from a case reported some years ago. The judge, not unnaturally, wants to be satisfied that the passage still accurately reflects the law. This question is essentially a straightforward factual inquiry, to which you should have the answer if your legal research was sufficiently thorough.

Questions about your argument

Judges often ask mooters to explain their arguments in more detail, usually because they do not entirely understand the point being made. A judge might phrase this sort of question in one of the following ways:

▶ 11.9

● **"What is the proposition that you derive from this authority?"**
Whenever you refer the judge to an authority, you should state the legal principle that you derive from it.[4] If you are not explicit, this question is frequently the result. You ought to know off the top of your head why you are relying on each of your authorities, so you should be able to answer this question without difficulty.

● **"If I understand you correctly, your submission is that . . . Is that right?"**
If a judge asks you this question, the chances are that he or she is struggling to understand a point you are making or to see where it is going. Listen carefully to the reformulation of your submission. Do not agree with it unless you are confident that it is accurate. If the judge has got something wrong, do not be afraid to say so.

Hostile questions

This type of question is intended to test or contradict one of your arguments. Hostile questions usually focus on perceived weaknesses in your case or points made by your opponents. Such interventions might take one of the following forms:

▶ 11.10

● **"Isn't there some force in your opponents' point that . . . ?"**
Just because the judge asks you this question, do not assume that he or she disagrees with your argument; it is simply another way of testing how persuasive you can be "off the cuff". Spending time before the moot thinking about how to counter your opponents' arguments will give you the edge when answering this type of question.

● **"Why should I prefer your authority to your opponents'?"**
An authority that you have cited may appear to conflict with an authority cited by your opponents. The judge may want to know why yours is preferable. In response, explain why your opponents' authority can be distinguished from the facts of the moot problem. Your notes should include a list of the main distinguishing factors.

---

4   Ch.10 explains the steps involved in referring judges to authorities.

● **"What do you say should happen in the following circumstances: . . . ?"**
With this type of question, the judge is attempting to apply the reasoning you are advocating to a different, and usually less helpful, set of circumstances. By testing the soundness of your argument, the judge will examine your familiarity with the material and your ability to think on your feet. The more you have thought through your arguments and the practical consequences of them, the easier you will find it to answer this sort of question. Take your time, however, and avoid suggesting a conclusion that is absurd.

Friendly questions

11.11 ▶ Judges sometimes ask benign questions. They may wish to help a mooter whose submissions have stalled or to ensure that every mooter is asked something. Friendly questions are generally easy to answer as long as you recognise them for what they are. Do not therefore assume that every question is hostile and get into an argument with a judge who is not actually trying to be difficult.

If the judge asks a friendly question, for example raising a good point you had not thought of, try to weave a reference to it into your speech. Not unnaturally, judges tend to be rather fond of the points they think of themselves and there is no harm in repeating them. You might do so by saying as follows: "As Your Lordship pointed out earlier in my submissions, . . ."

QUESTIONS YOU CANNOT ANSWER

11.12 ▶ Even if you have prepared meticulously for the moot and follow the practical guidance provided above, the judge may still ask a question that stumps you. If you find yourself in this position, do your best not to let it unnerve you. Even the most eminent QCs are faced every now and then with questions that leave them scratching their heads.

When the judge asks you a question you cannot answer directly, you must still provide a response of some sort. And you will not have much time in which to give it. The paragraphs below suggest what you can do in those circumstances.

Consult your team-mate

11.13 ▶ If you believe that your mooting partner may be able to answer the question, glance in his or her direction. A quick look should tell you whether or not your team-mate can help. If so, and before you engage in a protracted bout of stage whispers, ask the judge for permission to consult your team-mate. You might do so by saying, "My Lord, may I please briefly speak to my learned friend?" Few judges will refuse such a request.

This strategy can work well when the judge requests information or clarification that you are unable to provide. If your mooting partner can help, the two of you will demonstrate admirable teamwork by producing the answer. This approach works less well when the judge's intervention hits a weak spot in your argument. The judge will expect you to be able to defend your argument without first having to consult your team-mate.

Leave the question for your team-mate to answer

11.14 ▶ If your team-mate is still to speak, you can say to the judge, "My learned friend will address this point in his/her submissions". Your team-mate will then have a few minutes in which to formulate a response, which should consequently be an improvement on whatever you might come up with on the spur of the moment. This approach again works best when the judge requests specific information or clarification that you are unable to provide.

Before taking this route, you must, of course, ensure—perhaps with a quick sideways glance—that your team-mate is happy to take on the task of providing a response. What you cannot do is lumber your team-mate with responsibility for dealing with a stinker of a question that he or she is no better placed to answer than you.

Salvage what you can

If the judge asks a question that neither you nor your mooting partner can answer, try nonetheless to offer *something* positive by way of a response. Suppose, for example, that the judge asks whether you have considered the implications of a particular reported decision not cited at the moot. Although you have heard of the case, you have not read it and your team-mate looks non-plussed. One option would be to tell the judge point-blank, "My Lord, I am afraid that I have not read that case and cannot therefore assist." This response would inevitably appear weak. A more positive answer might look like this: "My Lord, I am not familiar with the detail of that case, but on this issue I rely on the decision in [refer to an authority that you *have* cited] and my learned friends opposite have not cited any authority that undermines it."

▶ 11.15

This example involves a request for information, but the same principle applies if the judge's intervention hits a weakness in one of your arguments. If you are conversant with the materials, you should be able to return fire, however weakly. For example, if the judge points out that your argument would lead to an unfortunate result in a particular scenario, consider whether the same result would follow if your opponents' solution were adopted. If so, you could say to the judge, "I see the force of Your Lordship's point, but precisely the same problem arises if Your Lordship accepts the submission of my learned friends opposite." Your ability to make the best of a "bad lot" will, of course, improve with experience.

Move (swiftly) on

There will be occasions when, despite your best efforts to answer a question, the judge remains visibly unpersuaded. In that event—which is just about your worst-case scenario—move on to your next submission as swiftly as you can. You might do so with these words: "My Lord, that is my submission/I cannot take this point any farther. With Your Lordship's permission, I now intend to move on to my next point." An implicit admission of defeat it may be, but it will at least allow you to retreat with your dignity intact.

▶ 11.16

CHAPTER CHECKLIST

- Welcome judicial interventions because they provide your best opportunity to impress the judge.
- Prepare for judicial interventions before the moot by identifying the topics that the judge's questions are most likely to focus on and by drafting notes that address those topics.
- When the judge asks a question:
  - Listen carefully.

▶ 11.17

- – Ask the judge to repeat anything you do not understand.
- – Provide an immediate response.
- – Maintain your public speaking technique while you answer.
- Review the list of stock questions contained in this chapter and make sure you are prepared to answer all of them.
- If you cannot answer a question, seek help from your team-mate, provide whatever sensible response you can and, if all else fails, move on to your next point.

12

Delivery

While the last two chapters examined what you should say during your oral submissions—the words that you use—this chapter is primarily concerned with how you should say it. The chapter begins with a short explanation of the importance of delivery in mooting before providing several suggestions for developing an effective style of delivery. The chapter ends with some advice on coping with nerves, an affliction that can have a detrimental impact on any mooter's delivery.

▶ 12.1

IMPORTANCE OF DELIVERY

The Classical Athenian statesman and orator Demosthenes was once asked to name the three most important parts of oratory. He reputedly replied, "*Delivery. Delivery. Delivery.*" Moot court advocacy is a form of oratory. The subject matter of a moot may be more technical than most political speeches and the setting for moots more stylised than for most debates, but the fundamental features are the same: mooters, like other orators, present arguments out loud to audiences they are trying to persuade.

▶ 12.2

Good delivery is essential for effective moot court advocacy for several reasons. First, it enables the mooter to communicate arguments to the judge. If the judge cannot hear or understand what a mooter is saying, the most brilliant arguments will fall on deaf ears. Second, good delivery ensures that the judge concentrates on what the mooter is saying. An audible and comprehensible argument may still fail to hit home if the judge is distracted by some aspect of the mooter's behaviour. Third, good delivery conveys the mooter's emotions to the judge. We are not talking about unalloyed joy or anger here, but subtler emotions. In particular, mooters must try to communicate two feelings at all times: self-confidence and belief in what they are saying.

In short, while Demosthenes may have slightly over-egged the pudding, no doubt to good rhetorical effect, he was essentially right. However thoroughly you research the moot problem, however immaculate your court dress and however compelling your arguments, you will not win the moot if you do not deliver your speech effectively.

DEVELOPING EFFECTIVE DELIVERY

For some reason, the perception exists that good public speakers are born, not made; that they owe their skills entirely to genetic good fortune. Little could be farther from the truth. Almost

▶ 12.3

anyone can learn how to deliver speeches effectively. You just need to work at it. If you require proof that public speaking can be taught, dip into the vast literature on the subject, starting with Aristotle's *On Rhetoric* in about 330 BC. Drawing on some of that literature, the next few pages contain several suggestions for developing good delivery. They examine three factors: your body; your voice; and your personality.

Body

12.4 ▶ Your body can communicate a range of messages—positive and negative—without you uttering a word. Three aspects of bodily communication are considered below. Each is central to effective moot court advocacy.

Eye contact

12.5 ▶ Your eyes are your most potent means of non-verbal communication. Use them in mooting by looking directly at the judge as often and for as long as you can. Start as you mean to go on: look the judge in the eyes when you stand up to begin your submissions and smile briefly. Then, speak as though you are engaging the judge in a conversation. When you have conversations with friends, you do not direct your remarks to a point six inches above their heads or to floor-boards beneath your feet. You look them in the eyes. Do the same with the judge. If you hold the judge's gaze, he or she will have no option but to concentrate on what you are saying.

Regular eye contact will also enable you to watch what the judge is doing. Does the judge look lost? You need to know. If the judge appears not to be following a particular submission, you may have to repeat or rephrase it. Looking up frequently will also enable you to see when the judge is writing something down. You can then wait for the judge's pen to stop moving before you launch into your next point.

If your moot tribunal consists of more than one judge, make eye contact with each of them separately. You are, in effect, addressing a small audience. Every member of that audience must be fully engaged with what you are saying.

Stance

12.6 ▶ Your stance is the way you stand when you deliver your speech. There are not too many ways in which mooting resembles golf, but stance is one of them. Just as you must address a golf ball using the correct stance, so you must adopt the right posture to address a moot judge. If you are slouched over your papers with your face directed at your feet, you will not only fail to project your voice, you will also give the judge the impression that you lack confidence in what you are saying. In such a position, there is little chance of sending your submissions safely down the middle of the mooting fairway.

There is nothing complicated about adopting a proper stance. Stick to the following guidelines and you will not go far wrong:

- Stand straight or lean very slightly forward from the waist.
- Hold your head up, even if you are looking down.
- Push your shoulders back so that you do not appear hunched.
- Keep your hands down. If you are holding your notes in front of you, your hands should be somewhere around the level of your waistband. Never put your hands in your pockets. It is too casual.

● If there is a lectern, by all means rest your hands on it. But the operative word is "rest". Do not put any weight on the lectern and avoid gripping both sides of it or you will look as though you are at the wheel of a four-ton lorry.

Gestures

A gesture in this context is a movement of the body. Gestures can add emphasis and colour to speeches, and convey a speaker's personality. However, excessive or inappropriate gesturing tends to distract the audience from what the speaker is saying.   ▶ 12.7

When you speak at moots, make your gestures deliberate and natural. Deliberate gestures are purposeful. You must therefore work to eradicate any unconscious movements and fidgeting. If you are prone, for example, to clicking your pen on and off or twiddling it in your fingers as you speak, force yourself not to pick it up in the first place. If you have a tendency to scratch the side of your nose, shoot your cuffs or play with a ring on your finger, put your hands to work holding your speaking notes.

Natural gestures reflect what you are saying. They emphasise particular points and are not excessively theatrical. So, for example, if you use the expression, "on the one hand, . . . on the other hand, . . .", you might open one hand in front of you and then the other as you speak. Similarly, if you emphasise a single thing (as in the sentence, "the authority my learned friend cites is only relevant in *one* respect"), you might raise an index finger as you utter the stressed word.

Voice

Your voice communicates your arguments to the judge. It must be audible, comprehensible and engaging. Four aspects of your voice largely control those qualities: volume, enunciation, pace and tone.   ▶ 12.8

Volume

If judges are to follow your oral submissions, they have to hear them. You must therefore speak loudly enough for your voice to carry across the moot courtroom. There is no need to deliver your speech in a booming basso-profondo. Just make a conscious effort to speak at a higher volume than you ordinarily would in conversation and to project your voice from your lungs rather than from your throat.   ▶ 12.9

And remember this: whilst judges frequently complain that the mooters who appear before them speak too softly, you will be almost unique in the annals of mooting history if a judge criticises you for speaking too loudly.

Enunciation

You must pronounce your words clearly so that the judge understands what you are saying. There is no need to go overboard, however. Speak naturally, but pronounce every syllable and do not swallow the ends of your words.   ▶ 12.10

Pace

The pace of your delivery is the speed at which you speak. Many mooters speak too quickly. The adrenaline that their bodies produce misleads their brains into thinking that they are talking at   ▶ 12.11

a normal conversational pace when they are actually galloping through their submissions like a horse-racing commentator as the field enters the final furlong.

This hormonal deception has several unfortunate consequences. For one thing, mooters who speak too quickly sound nervous, even if they are not. More importantly, oral submissions delivered at breakneck pace lose much of their potency because judges struggle to follow them.

You should therefore remind yourself repeatedly to slow down. If it helps, write the words "slow down" at the top of every page of your notes. It is possible to speak too slowly, so guard against it. But speaking too quickly is by far the more common affliction.

Now and again, you should not be afraid to bring your delivery to a complete stand-still. A short silence—and, be warned, the shortest silence will seem like an age to you—will quickly grab the judge's attention if you are worried that his or her mind is drifting from the point you are making. A moment's silence is also a useful way of adding emphasis if it follows immediately after a particularly important submission.

Tone

12.12 ▶ Tone refers to the modulation of the voice—the accents that the speaker puts on particular words and phrases. If you deliver your oral submissions in a flat monotone, the judge will quickly lose interest in what you are saying.

Vary the tone of your voice regularly. The variations must sound natural, however. Place emphasis only on words that merit it, just as you would when you speak casually with friends. Try, therefore, to avoid what linguists call "Australian questioning intonation", whereby the tone of the voice rises at the end of each sentence to the level of a question even though no question is being asked. It is not natural. Unless, that is, you are Australian.

Personality

12.13 ▶ Within the confines outlined above, develop a style of delivery that suits your personality. In other words, be yourself. A becoming style is persuasive because it is sincere and the speaker feels comfortable using it. An unnatural style, by contrast, looks forced and occasionally ridiculous.

Even if you are naturally soft-spoken and diffident, your personality should dictate your style of delivery and not the other way round. Make virtues of your personality traits. Speak in a calm and measured way, and let your knowledge of the material and the persuasive force of your arguments impress the judge. Just make sure that you keep your voice up and look the judge in the eyes whenever possible.

COPING WITH NERVES

12.14 ▶ Virtually all mooters suffer from nerves or performance anxiety at some point. Nerves affect different people in different ways, but there are several classic symptoms: sweaty palms; shaky hands; wobbles in the lower intestines; uncontrollable yawns; and speaking too quickly. Some people's nerves disappear as soon as they stand up to speak. Others are not so lucky.

A severe bout of nerves can have a debilitating effect on delivery. Aside from appearing nervous — never a good look when you are on your feet — sufferers tend to garble their words and become flustered when asked the most straightforward questions.

Any anxiety you feel about mooting will naturally diminish over time as your experience grows. In the meantime, use the following strategies to cope with your nerves before and during moots.

Prepare thoroughly

At the heart of most people's nervousness about mooting is a fear of the unknown, particularly the questions the judge will ask. The best way to minimise that fear is to prepare thoroughly for moots. The better you understand the relevant law and the more you have thought through the arguments on both sides, the less likely it is that the judge will ask you a question you cannot answer. If you have prepared properly, you can also rationally tell yourself that you have nothing to be afraid of; you have worked hard and you know your stuff.

⯈ 12.15

    If you are a novice mooter, part of the uncertainty of mooting is not knowing what a moot courtroom looks like. Reading Ch.8 should give you an idea, but there is no substitute for paying a visit to the room that will be your moot court. Familiarise yourself with its layout and, if you can, try out the acoustics at the spot from which you will speak.

Embrace fear

Keep in mind that a certain level of fear is good. It indicates that adrenaline is pumping through your body. Adrenaline will increase your energy levels, sharpen your wits and improve your performance at the moot. Remember also that people rarely look as nervous as they feel. Even if you are wracked with worry, you probably do not look it.

⯈ 12.16

Get angry

Most people find that their anxiety level drops when they get angry. So get irritated. Not apoplectic with rage, just mildly annoyed. Do so by empathising with your "client". In mooting, unlike professional practice, your client is imaginary, but you can still work yourself up into a state of righteous indignation on your client's behalf. You simply have to suspend disbelief a little.

⯈ 12.17

    Think back to the illustrative moot problem. Say you were acting for the appellant, Mr Dickens. Put yourself in his shoes. He would be very angry about what had happened. Mr Cecil used to be his friend. In a spirit of friendship, Mr Dickens provided some free advice. And look how Mr Cecil repaid him! By suing Mr Dickens for an enormous sum of money and dragging him through the courts.

    You could get just as worked up on Mr Cecil's behalf. He would also feel betrayed by his former friend. Mr Dickens knew that Mr Cecil was not a lawyer and would have no idea about limitation periods. Mr Dickens's failure to mention the limitation period has cost Mr Cecil a fortune.

    Remember, though, that getting angry in the sense described here is a form of motivation. It should not spill into showing anger at the moot toward your opponents or the judge.

Keep a sense of perspective

Although you might feel as if you are suffering from the world's worst case of moot-induced nervous paralysis, try to see the bigger picture. First, you are going through nothing more than

⯈ 12.18

countless others have experienced before you and will experience after you. Even most practising advocates regularly suffer from nerves. Second, you are not expected to scale the heights of oratorical brilliance during your moot speech. If you demonstrate competence, show a good understanding of the moot problem and the relevant law, and articulate your points comprehensibly and clearly, you will impress the judge and the audience.

CHAPTER CHECKLIST

12.19

- Develop a style of delivery that suits your personality.
- Whatever your style of delivery:
    - Maintain eye contact with the judge for as much of your speech as possible.
    - Stand straight when you speak with your head up, your shoulders back and your hands down.
    - Make natural gestures and eliminate unconscious habits and fidgeting.
    - Speak loudly enough for the judge to hear clearly everything you say.
    - Enunciate your words properly.
    - Speak slowly.
    - Vary the tone of your voice regularly.
- To cope with nerves:
    - Prepare as thoroughly as possible for the moot.
    - Embrace fear.
    - Get (mildly) angry by empathising with your "client".
    - Keep a sense of perspective.

Organising

"Don't agonize, organize."

Florynce Kennedy, US civil-rights advocate (1916–2000)

▶ 13
Organising moots

Whilst the bulk of this book is geared towards those who wish to participate in moots, the next three chapters are directed at those who wish to organise them. (There may, of course, be an overlap between the two.) You may, for example, be a law lecturer who wishes to set up a mooting competition as an adjunct to classes on advocacy and civil procedure. Or you may be an undergraduate law student who wants to set up a mooting society. In either event, this chapter should be of interest to you. ▶ 13.1

Organisation is vital to the success of any mooting competition. A well organised competition will generate the goodwill of the supporting institution and attract both participants and judges who will know that they are not wasting their time by taking part. In contrast, a badly organised competition tends to erode goodwill, whether of the supporting institution, the contestants or the judges, in some cases to the point where it is impossible for the competition to survive.

The extent of the assistance that you need to organise a mooting competition will, of course, depend on what, if any, arrangements you inherit. The next three chapters will not therefore be relevant to everyone who sets out to organise a mooting competition. If a competition already exists at the institution where you are based, there should, for example, be little need for you to read about how to draft a set of rules. Similarly, if you are fortunate enough to have at your disposal a large number of good quality mooting problems, the chapter on selecting and writing moot problems may be surplus to your requirements.

INITIAL CONSIDERATIONS

Once you have resolved to run a mooting competition, it is necessary to make some basic decisions about its organisation. In particular, you must determine how to structure it and who will be eligible to take part. A number of considerations also arise in scheduling moots. This section will examine each of these issues in turn. ▶ 13.2

Structure of the competition
There are two basic models for mooting competitions, which, to use a sporting analogy, may be termed "knockout" and "Champions League". The former is far more common than the latter. Both of these structures are described below, as is one of the fundamental concerns for the organiser of any mooting competition: who wins? There is then a short discussion of non-competitive or ad hoc moots. ▶ 13.3

"Knockout" competitions

13.4 In this model, students are placed into a pyramidal draw with a series of preliminary rounds, quarter-finals, semi-finals and a final, with the winning mooters from each "match" going through to the next round. This format is readily understood, relatively easy to organise and motivating for students who know that they must win every round to progress. It also requires less resource, in terms of rooms and judges, as the competition progresses. The primary disadvantage of "knockout" mooting competitions is that first-round losers do not have the opportunity to compete in a second moot unless there is some form of repechage. This can be particularly unfortunate for those, potentially able, mooters who find themselves on the wrong end of a first-round decision. The organiser of a "knockout" competition may also be faced with logistical difficulties if the number of entrants does not precisely fit the "pyramid". In those circumstances, some mooters will probably have to be given byes to the second round, which may put them at a competitive disadvantage when they have to moot against a team that has mooted before.

"Champions League" competitions

13.5 Under this format, teams are placed into groups (usually of four) and each team moots in successive rounds against every other team in the group. The team with the greatest number of wins then goes forward to a short "knockout" phase that concludes with the final.

The major advantage of the "Champions League" format is that each team is guaranteed to moot more than once, so ensuring that the participants can focus on developing their mooting skills rather than on winning their first moot at all costs. This format is very intensive, however, in terms of the numbers of rooms and judges required because teams are not eliminated after each round. There may also be some students who do not wish to moot as many as two or three times and who will accordingly be put off by the commitment involved. From an organisational perspective, another concern is that there may be more than one team with the same number of wins after the "group stage" is completed. In that event, it will be necessary to come up with some way of deciding who goes through to the "knockout" rounds. Finally, you may run into logistical problems if the number of teams is not divisible by the number of groups, particularly as, unlike "knockout" competitions, it is not possible to grant byes.

Who wins the moot?

13.6 Whether you adopt a "Knockout" or "Champions League" format for your competition, every moot requires a winner. You must therefore make a basic policy decision at the outset as to whether the winner will be the best team or the two best individual mooters regardless of whether or not they are on the same team.

The vast majority of mooting competitions put forward the best team and this is the only workable approach for a "Champions League" competition. Putting the best team through has a number of merits, not the least of which is that it encourages teamwork between the mooters, for example in conducting research and assisting with judicial interventions. It also mirrors professional practice, in which it is the combined efforts of the advocates acting on behalf of each party that win the day; the court does not differentiate between leading counsel for the appellant and junior counsel for the respondent.

It may nonetheless be worth at least considering the alternative of awarding the moot to the two best individual advocates. Perhaps surprisingly, some students actively encourage this approach. Their argument is usually based on the perceived unfairness of an outstanding mooter being eliminated from the competition because his or her partner is not up to scratch. This refrain is typically heard from first year law undergraduates and postgraduate students who may know very little about their chosen partners when they enter the competition. It can also be a bugbear of students who have entered the competition individually and been paired up randomly by the organiser with another lone entrant. Additionally, there is the fair point that, for those intent on entering the ranks of the profession, working with a range of different partners is a skill worth acquiring.

Ad hoc moots

It is possible to organise moots on an ad hoc basis, outside the confines of a structured competition. This format can be a useful alternative if there are too few students with a sustained interest in mooting to justify a formal competition. It can also be encouraged amongst students who have been knocked out of a formal competition, but wish nevertheless to gain additional mooting experience.   ▶ 13.7

The obligations on the organiser of ad hoc moots are obviously reduced. Once the participants are identified and arranged into teams, dates can be offered with "fixtures" emerging as teams declare themselves available on any given occasion. The organiser must then supply a venue, a moot problem and, of course, a judge.

The advantage of this model is its flexibility. It can accommodate students who wish to moot only once. It can also work for those mooters who have mooted before, but wish to have another go. The great disadvantage of ad hoc mooting is that students tend, unsurprisingly, to be far less motivated than when they moot in a structured competition. This can result in inconsistent levels of preparation and regular postponements.

ELIGIBILITY TO COMPETE

The organiser must decide who is eligible to take part before the competition begins. There are two primary considerations to bear in mind when you make this decision: the need to ensure that there is a reasonably level playing field for all of the contestants; and the adequacy of the resources at your disposal. Both of these considerations are discussed below.   ▶ 13.8

Maintaining a level playing field

Most law faculties run different academic programmes that attract students of varying ages and experience. Many, for example, offer undergraduate and postgraduate law degrees, as well as postgraduate vocational courses. Some English institutions teach the Graduate Diploma in Law alongside LPC and BPTC vocational courses. There is a risk that allowing students from different programmes to moot against one another will give the more experienced students a competitive advantage. In particular, students on vocational courses will usually have completed undergraduate law degrees and might therefore already have mooting experience. They will also be in the midst of a skills course that specifically teaches advocacy.   ▶ 13.9

The moot organiser must decide whether these factors will render the mooting competition unfair if it is open to everyone. The selection criteria are a matter of judgment for the organiser based on the make-up of the student body, the likely interest from different elements of it and the curriculum. The organiser will have to accept that there will always be an uneven playing surface to some extent. Even if eligibility is restricted to undergraduates, for example, the final-year students will enjoy an advantage over their juniors.

If the organiser takes the view that the discrepancies between the various parts of the student body will render the competition unfair if all can compete against each other, there are at least two available options. The first, if resources permit, is to run two separate competitions, one for "novices" and another for those with previous mooting experience. The second option is to restrict entry to the competition, for example by limiting it to students at a particular level (say, undergraduates other than those in their first year).

Adequacy of resources

13.10 ▷ Mooting requires considerable resources. Every four mooters (assuming two teams of two per moot) require a room and at least one judge for a period of as much as an hour and a half. The resources that you can bring to bear may accordingly restrict the maximum number of moots that you can run on a single night. This, in turn, is likely to affect the maximum number of students that your competition can accommodate.

You may find that the interest in your competition outstrips the resources at your disposal. In that event, you will have to impose selection criteria. There is any number of possibilities including "first come, first served", pulling names out of a hat and favouring more senior students who are in the midst of job applications and need the experience. Whichever mechanism you use, it is important to let the eligible students know as early as possible in the academic year so that you are not faced with complaints of unfairness. If resources allow, you may be able to placate disappointed students by offering them some form of ad hoc mooting.

A strategy for limiting numbers

13.11 ▷ Students sometimes happily sign up to participate in mooting competitions without fully appreciating what is involved. This can have a deleterious effect on the competition if swathes of participants drop out after it has started. As a moot organiser, you need to bear this risk in mind and do what you can to minimise it.

One way of impressing on students the commitment involved in mooting is to insist that all potential participants attend an initial briefing if they wish to be considered for entry into the competition. The briefing will enable you to explain in detail to students what mooting involves. It is likely that only the more motivated will then sign up for the competition with the more "flaky" potential mooters dropping by the wayside in a process of self-selection.

If you do go down this route, your briefing might include a short explanation of what mooting is and how your competition will work, a description on a task-by-task basis of what the contestants will have to do in the lead up to each moot and a word or two about the judging, identifying for example, who the judges are likely to be and the criteria that they will use to determine who wins each moot. You might round off by inviting questions from the floor and, of course, heartily recommending to those assembled that they buy a copy of this book.

Scheduling considerations

Once you have decided on a structure for your mooting competition, you can start thinking about when each round will take place. Your schedule will have to take account of the limitations that afflict all institutions, including term dates and the availability of rooms.

▶ 13.12

It is vital when picking dates for moots to factor in the level of student workload for curricular activities. Ideally, you want to choose less intensive periods for your moots so that the students and judges have adequate time to prepare. You should also have regard to any dates for handing in assessments and try to ensure that they do not fall during the week before or the week after a moot.

DRAFTING RULES FOR MOOTING COMPETITIONS

Whatever the structure of your competition, it will require a set of rules to give the participants the confidence that it is organised in a fair and transparent way. In any event, since mooting by its very nature tends to attract the more argumentative students, it is as well to pre-empt any disagreements with a clear set of rules.

▶ 13.13

There is a specimen set of rules at Appendix I, which you are free to adopt and modify. You may, however, want to draft a fresh set of rules to reflect your own circumstances. If you do, the following are probably the most important questions to consider:

● **Who will be eligible to take part in the competition?**
Is it to be restricted to undergraduate students or will it be opened up to graduate students as well? Is it to be limited to a particular class of students, such as those in their final year of study? If relevant, can students on vocational courses participate?

● **The format of the competition**
Will you employ a "Knockout" or "Champions League" format? If the latter, how will you resolve any tie at the end of the group stage?

● **Who will win the moot?**
Should the best team or the two best individual mooters win the moot?

● **Judging the moot**
How many judges will you have for each moot? Normally, one will suffice, although you may wish to have two or three in the later rounds. You must also decide whether to have written judging criteria or whether the decision should be left entirely to the discretion of the judges. In many competitions, the judges are asked to award points to the teams based on a number of identified factors. The team (or two individual mooters if this is the system that is chosen) with the greatest number of points wins the moot. If you have devised a points system, you should consider incorporating it into the competition rules. There is a sample judge's score sheet at Appendix II.

● Skeleton arguments

Will the teams be obliged to produce skeleton arguments? If so, will you impose a word or page limit on each skeleton? How will you ensure that the parties exchange skeleton arguments and that you receive copies for the judge? What will the deadline for exchange be?

● The number of authorities that each team can cite

Will you impose a restriction on the number of authorities that each team can cite? It is usually a good idea to do so if you are to avoid mooters submitting long lists of authorities, many of which they will be unable to refer to at the moot. If you impose a limit, you may wish to define what constitutes an authority. Will statutes, statutory instruments, textbooks and articles count? You may also wish to clarify whether cases referred to within reported decisions are themselves to count as separate authorities. This point comes up quite frequently. The sample rules in Appendix I deal with it by explaining that the mere recitation of an extract from case B that appears in case A does not make case B an additional authority.

● Should contestants be required to collate their authorities in a bundle?

The benefits of preparing bundles of authorities are discussed in Ch.6. You may consider that those benefits are sufficient to justify requiring each team to produce a bundle in advance of every moot. The preparation of bundles does, of course, involve a certain level of added expense for the participants. Bundles are also time-consuming to produce. You might therefore consider imposing a requirement to produce a bundle only from a late stage of the competition, say the semi-final.

● The format of authorities

Are you happy for the contestants to print off copies of their authorities from online databases such as Westlaw UK, LexisNexis and Lawtel or should they be required to produce photocopies of the relevant law reports for the judge? Printing the online versions of case reports is likely to be cheaper and easier for students, but may not carry the authoritativeness or user-friendliness of a hard copy report (for example, if the submissions of counsel are missing or there are no paragraph numbers). Much will depend on the size of your competition and whether your law library stocks multiple sets of hard copy law reports.

● Running order and timing

Your rules should state the order in which the mooters will speak. They should also identify the time limits on each mooter and make it clear whether those limits are inclusive or exclusive of time spent dealing with judicial interventions.

● Reservation of powers to the competition organiser

You will normally want to stipulate that the organiser has the right to amend the rules and that any decision that he or she makes about the rules and their interpretation will be final.

OBTAINING SPONSORSHIP

Some mooting competitions are sponsored by local practising lawyers. Obtaining sponsorship can enhance the quality of a competition in a number of respects. First and foremost, if the competition is associated with the legal profession, it is likely to reinforce in the eyes of the contestants how mooting can act as a bridge between education and practice; the competition is not just an offshoot of the curriculum, but has a real connection with practising the law. This tends to act as a powerful motivator for students. ▶ 13.14

Second, the sponsors are usually able to provide judges for the later rounds of the competition and possibly one or two practitioners who are prepared to give a mooting masterclass.[1] The involvement of practitioners not only provides diversity and expertise amongst the judges, it also motivates students who feel (rightly) that, if they can impress practitioner judges, they can make the grade as professional advocates.

Finally, it is likely that the sponsor will make some form of financial contribution to the competition. These funds may be used to defray the running costs of the competition or to produce a larger prize for the winners than would otherwise be possible.

Whom to approach

In general, you are more likely to be successful with a local potential sponsor. Your institution may already have a relationship with local practitioners, for example through their attending advisory panels or careers fairs. You should start with them. You should also bear in mind that there ought to be some correlation between the legal practice(s) that you approach and the likely subject matter of most of your moot problems. If, for example, your mooting competition will exclusively feature civil law problems, it may not be sensible to seek sponsorship from a law firm or barristers' chambers that only practises criminal law. ▶ 13.15

How to approach potential sponsors

It is important that you explain clearly and succinctly to potential sponsors what you are looking for as well as the advantages to them in getting involved. You might start by producing a short letter summarising three key points: how the competition will work; what you would like from the sponsor; and what you perceive to be the advantages to the sponsor. Set out below is a little more detail about the sort of information that you could include on each of these three points. ▶ 13.16

How the competition will work

You might explain how many students are involved in the competition, the academic programme (or programmes) that those students are undertaking, the proposed structure of the competition and any key organisational features (such as whether skeleton arguments are required). Information of this nature should impress on potential sponsors that your mooting competition is well organised and worthy of support.

---

[1]   Masterclasses are discussed later in this chapter.

What you would like from the sponsor

Your wish list is likely to include some or all of the following: use of the sponsor's name on promotional materials; a cash sum to contribute towards the running costs and/or prizes; possibly, a prize in the form of a guaranteed spot on a vacation placement or mini-pupillage scheme; the provision of judges for the later rounds of the competition; and a commitment to conduct a mooting masterclass.

The advantages to the sponsor

Most practitioners are only too aware of the need to market themselves effectively to students with a view to optimising their recruitment programmes. Involvement in mooting can enable practitioners to put themselves across in a more focused and interactive fashion than at a formal marketing event. The opportunities are greatest if there is going to be a pre-moot masterclass or a post-moot social gathering or prize-giving.

PUBLICISING MOOTING COMPETITIONS

13.17 ▶ Publicity can play an important part in the success of a mooting competition. Before the competition is launched, the role of publicity is to inform students of its existence and to encourage as many students as possible to sign up. Once the competition is up and running, the primary object of publicity is to maximise the number of spectators at each moot. Good publicity, whether before or after the competition has started, will raise the profile of the competition within the institution and attract the interest of students who are not directly involved. They may come along to watch moots out of curiosity or to support friends who are taking part. Well-judged publicity can also create a "feel-good" factor around the mooting competition, bringing it into the mainstream of student life.

Pre-launch publicity

13.18 ▶ A poster campaign is the most obvious way of raising awareness amongst students before a mooting competition gets under way. It is often more effective to use your posters to promote a message suggestive of what mooting is about (such as persuasion or verbal duelling) than to rely on an anodyne "would you like to join the mooting society?"

   If your finances permit, you should consider producing a short brochure that you can distribute to all interested students at the freshers' fair and elsewhere. The brochure might explain briefly what mooting is and what its benefits are, provide details of the structure of the competition that you have organised and the dates on which moots will take place, and explain what further steps students need to take if they wish to sign up. You will find sample text for such a brochure at Appendix III.

   To ensure maximum coverage, it is advisable to ask lecturers either to make an announcement or to show a publicity slide at the start of their classes. Additionally, if your institution has a newsletter or intranet, do not pass up the opportunity to advertise there. If you are beginning to feel uneasy that this approach has more in common with ambush marketing than restrained academic publicity, rest assured that, no matter how hard you try, there will always be some students who complain that they were not made aware at the start of the term that they could moot.

Post-launch publicity

The role of publicity after the competition is in train is principally to advertise when and where each moot is taking place, and to make it clear that spectators are welcome. When advertising the dates and locations of moots, you might consider making use of whatever student newsletter your institution runs. Your publicity might also mention the names of the contestants and judges, and the subject matter of the moot (e.g. contract or tort/delict). You could even reproduce the whole moot problem if you have space.

▶ 13.19

SELECTING AND BRIEFING THE JUDGES

The quality of the judging and, in particular, of the feedback that the judges give to the mooters is integral to the success of a mooting competition. It is therefore critical to put some time and effort into selecting and briefing the judges involved in your competition.

▶ 13.20

Selecting judges

There are broadly three categories of judges: students; members of the academic staff at your institution; and practitioners. Each category is discussed below.

▶ 13.21

Students

Unless you are running a very small mooting competition, it is likely that you will make some use of students as judges. For many competitions, they will be the most common source of judicial material.

▶ 13.22

The principal advantage of student judges is their availability. Many students, particularly ex-mooters, are only too happy to subject their peers to judicial scrutiny. Availability is not the only advantage of student judges, however. They will usually understand more acutely than other types of judge what the participants are going through. They are accordingly often able to provide perceptive and comprehensible feedback.

The principal drawback of student judges is that they tend to lack the gravitas of academics and practitioners. As a result, there is a danger of the proceedings becoming too relaxed and informal.

Members of the academic staff

Using academics as judges has a number of advantages. As long as you are able to match the right members of staff to the right moots, they will have considerable knowledge of the subject area, which should facilitate some good interventions. Most members of staff are also able to adopt sufficient judicial airs to ensure that the moot is conducted with the requisite degree of seriousness. The flip-side of this is that some mooters find it difficult to adjust to members of the academic staff acting as judges. Some may even be concerned about performing in front of people who might be marking their exams at the end of the year.

▶ 13.23

None of this should dissuade you from using members of staff as judges. Indeed, the drawbacks referred to above are not dissimilar to the difficulties that advocates sometimes face in practice when they find themselves appearing before judges who were formerly colleagues. The one real disadvantage of calling on academics to act as judges is that their hours of work and domestic commitments may mean that they are not always available to judge in the evening, when most moots take place.

Practitioners

13.24 ▶ The most obvious advantage of using practitioners as judges is that they bring with them professional experience of the judicial process. They know how judges act and the feedback that they give will satisfy the desire of the participants to know how things are done in practice. One downside of using practitioners to judge your moots is that they tend to be even less available than members of staff and therefore need to be used more sparingly. It can also be quite intimidating for students to face practitioner judges. They are therefore generally best employed in the later rounds of mooting competitions.

Practitioners, of course, hail from a wide variety of backgrounds. The particular expertise of any given practitioner will to some extent govern what he or she brings to the mooting experience. The most obvious distinctions between practitioners are described below:

● **Judge or advocate**

Practising judges are clearly the best people to give definitive guidance on what does or does not persuade them. They often pick up on points that other types of moot judge are less concerned about, such as what to wear in court. The fortes of practising advocates, by contrast, are to guide students on how to prepare their cases, to explain the tricks of the advocate's trade and to prepare students for the different styles of judging that they are likely to encounter in practice.

● **Criminal or civil advocate**

Criminal advocates spend the majority of their working lives on their feet in court. As a result of this, and of the "blood and guts" nature of their practices, they usually have a fund of excellent tips for effective advocacy as well as a plethora of interesting courtroom "war stories". Although civil advocates are generally less well versed in the art of examining witnesses, they often have more experience of drafting skeleton arguments and making submissions on the law, both of which are key mooting skills.

● **Senior or junior advocate**

Senior advocates bring gravitas and experience to judging, but their very seniority can distance them from the average mooter. Junior advocates provide a closer reference point and students can usually relate to them more easily. They are also more likely to appear regularly in the types of court where mooters will begin their professional careers.

● **Advocate or litigation solicitor**

Litigation solicitors who do not themselves appear in court usually still have a well-developed sense of what to look for in an advocate, as well as a good stock of advocacy anecdotes. The principal disadvantage of using litigation solicitors as judges is that they will not be able to tell mooters how they would themselves deal with a particular point or difficulty.

Briefing judges

Whether your judges are students, academics or practitioners, it is important that you brief them adequately on how you want them to approach their task. A sensible option is to send your judges copies of a short written guidance note in advance of the moot. Appendix IV contains sample text for such a note. The note that you draft will, of course, have to reflect the rules of your competition. If you decide to write a briefing note from scratch, you should ensure that it covers the topics discussed below.

▶ 13.25

The system for judging

You will have to explain to the judges the system that you have chosen to determine the winners of the moot. If you have devised a points system, for example, your briefing note should identify each category that you are asking the judges to score, the maximum number of points available under each head and how many points you would award for excellent, good, average and poor performances. Without this latter indication, some judges may be naturally meaner or more generous than others when scoring. Maintaining consistency will then be very difficult.

▶ 13.26

The principal rules of the competition

You should draw the judges' attention in the briefing note to the most significant of the competition rules. Two good examples are the speaking time allotted to each mooter (making it clear whether this is exclusive or inclusive of time spent dealing with judicial interventions) and the maximum number of authorities on which each mooter is entitled to rely. You might also include some generic advice on how to deal with breaches of the rules by the participants. You could explain, for example, how the judges should deal with common defaults such as mooters running over their allotted speaking time or attempting to introduce authorities that have not been notified in advance of the moot.

▶ 13.27

Guidelines on judicial interventions

Intervention is a key area. If there is not enough of it, the moot becomes little more than a presentation and lacks the authenticity of the courtroom experience. Too much intervention and the moot can take on the aura of an exchange with the Spanish Inquisition. In order to strike a happy medium, you should consider advising judges to think about the following points when intervening:

▶ 13.28

● **Test the submission not the law**

The intervention should generally test the argument that the mooter makes rather than the mooter's wider knowledge of the law. For example, an intervention to the effect that, "if you take that submission to its logical conclusion, does it not mean [X]?" is fairer than an intervention along the lines of, "do you know of any other reported case in this area of the law that supports your submission?".

● **Ask each mooter roughly the same number of questions**

Each mooter should be subjected to approximately the same number of interventions. Save, perhaps, in the later rounds of the competition, when the mooters can reasonably expect to face more searching questions from the bench, judges should think in terms of making two or three significant interventions per mooter.

● Do not labour the point

Whilst mooters should be given every opportunity to answer questions from the bench, if they are obviously floundering, judges should encourage them to move on to another point. Although being moved along in this way can be a bit of a blow to the mooter's confidence, it is generally more palatable for all concerned (not least the audience) than an embarrassed and prolonged silence.

Guidelines on giving judgment

13.29 ▶ In the context of mooting, giving judgment is a two-stage process: a judgment on the law; and a judgment on the moot. Judges should be guided on both.

● Judgment on the law

The judgment on the law should be short, but reasoned. Given the amount of time that the contestants will have devoted to the moot problem, they are entitled to expect a sensible judgment. Some of the audience will also be interested in the rationale for the legal outcome. If there are going to be multiple judges on the moot bench, you might even suggest that one of them gives a short dissenting judgment. It can certainly add an element of levity to the proceedings.

● Judgment on the moot

Strictly speaking, the judgment on the moot is no more than the bare statement that one team (or two mooters) has won. It should, however, also include feedback on the strengths and weaknesses of the individual participants. Some judges prefer to announce who has won the moot before going on to give individual feedback. Others take the reverse approach. Either way works well, although waiting until the end to announce the result does have the advantage of ensuring that both teams listen attentively to the feedback.

Guidelines on giving feedback

13.30 ▶ Many students emphasise that it is the feedback that most helps them to reflect on their performances and improve their mooting skills. It is therefore important that your judges are well briefed on giving feedback. It may be worth, in particular, warning them to avoid either of the two extreme models for giving feedback. At the "right-wing" extreme are those judges who give a fully itemised breakdown of every error that each mooter made, from typos in the skeleton arguments to failing to wear a sufficiently conservative tie. At the "left-wing" extreme are those judges who favour generalised "pat on the back" feedback along the lines of, "both teams were very good, but team B was slightly better".

Neither of these extremes will help the mooters to improve. In order to achieve that objective, consider advising your judges to think about the following when giving feedback:

● **Focus on a small number of points**

Judges should restrict themselves to no more than two or three points of feedback. They should concentrate on those issues that will make the greatest difference to the overall standard of performance.

● **Start with positive feedback**

Judges should begin their feedback by giving an example of something that the mooter did well, rather than a biting criticism.

● **Give examples of problem areas and suggest solutions**

Negative feedback is generally the most valuable, but it must be handled with care. It can often assist if the judges are able to provide concrete examples of the errors that the mooters made. Having criticised a mooter's performance, a judge should always suggest how it could have been improved. The judge might say, for example, that, "You became confused about how to address the bench. You might try writing out the appropriate mode of address at the top of each page of your notes so that you always have it in front of you when you are speaking."

MOOTING MASTERCLASSES

Masterclasses are most often associated with the world of music, when distinguished musicians give advanced instruction on one or two selected compositions to eager audiences of students. In mooting terms, the purpose of a masterclass is very similar. An experienced practitioner, supported by the organiser of the mooting competition, seeks to develop specific mooting skills through a mixture of demonstration and critique. ▶ 13.31

Mooting masterclasses can take many forms, right up to a full mock moot between students or practitioners. It is important, however, that any masterclass that you run is pitched at an appropriate level that reflects how much your students know about mooting.

Two types of masterclass are described below: (1) an introduction to mooting; and, (2) a more advanced lesson in specific mooting skills. Both are mere examples. Any number of other topics may fit the bill.

Introductory masterclass

The purpose of an introductory masterclass is to explain in general terms what mooting involves. It might therefore take place before the first round of your mooting competition begins. Events of this type can be an excellent opportunity for junior practitioners to recount their own experiences and to emphasise how mooting helped them in practice. In many cases, practitioners are also happy to emphasise how mooting can assist students with job applications. ▶ 13.32

An introductory masterclass might include a straightforward interactive exercise, which gives students a flavour of what mooting involves as well as some guidance and feedback on the basic skills required. An example exercise of this sort is described in figure 13.1.

An exercise of this sort reflects the common mooting scenario in which the judge asks the mooter for a summary of the salient facts of a cited case. The exercise forces the students to focus on the central facts of the decision. It also puts them through the experience (in

13.33 ▶ **Figure 13.1:**
Introductory masterclass

> At the beginning of the masterclass, distribute the headnote from a well-known reported case and tell the students that they have five minutes to read it and make notes about it. Once the time expires, ask for volunteers to stand up and, in no more than one minute, summarise the facts of the case to the practitioner. The students should be told to address their remarks to the practitioner as if he or she were a judge.
>
> After each student's submissions, the practitioner should provide some brief feedback, concentrating in particular on stance, voice projection, eye contact and the appropriate use of language.

some cases for the first time) of listening to the sound of their own voices when making legal submissions in front of an audience.

Advanced masterclass

13.34 ▶ The aim of an advanced masterclass is to give students practical assistance in developing one or more higher level mooting skills. It typically takes place after the first round of a mooting competition, by which point the participants should already be familiar with the basics of mooting.

There is a wide variety of topics that you can use for an advanced masterclass. You could opt, for example, for a masterclass on devising an efficient research strategy or on dealing effectively with judicial interventions. You should generally choose the subject matter jointly with the practitioner who leads the masterclass since the professional background of your practitioner is likely to determine how he or she can best add value.

One possibility for an advanced masterclass is the effective use of skeleton arguments and authorities during oral submissions. These are two areas in which mooters often struggle and where practitioners can add real value. Set out in figure 13.2 is an example exercise of such a masterclass based on the illustrative case of *Cecil v Dickens*.

General considerations for organising masterclasses

13.35 ▶ There are three particular organisational considerations that you should bear in mind when organising masterclasses (whether introductory or advanced):

● **Timing and attendees**
You should schedule each masterclass to last for an hour and a half at most. This is, frankly, the limit of most students' attention spans. Provided that there is space to accommodate them, consider extending the invitation to all interested students rather than just those who are eligible to take part in the mooting competition.

● **Publicity**
To ensure maximum attendance, make sure that you publicise the masterclass appropriately. The same publicity machine that you employed to get the mooting competition noticed in the first place[2] can also be wheeled into action for this purpose.

---

[2] See the discussion of publicity earlier in this chapter.

Figure 13.2:
Advanced masterclass

▷ 13.36

A week or so before the masterclass is due to take place, distribute to the likely attendees copies of the moot problem in *Cecil v Dickens* together with short specimen skeleton arguments on behalf of both of the parties. The skeletons should deal with only one of the grounds of appeal and will have been drafted either by you or by the practitioner leading the masterclass. Ask the students to read the moot problem, the skeleton arguments and one of the reported cases cited in one of the skeleton arguments, and to prepare in advance of the masterclass a two-minute submission based on those materials for one side or the other. You should explain that the submission will be made to the practitioner, as if he or she were a judge, and that it must refer both to the relevant passage of the skeleton argument and to at least one passage from the reported case.

During the masterclass, volunteers should be sought to make submissions. It should be at the practitioner's discretion whether or not to intervene with questions. After each student has completed his submissions, the practitioner should provide brief feedback, focusing on how effectively the student managed to link the skeleton argument and the authority. The practitioner should also be prepared to give a short demonstration at the end of the session showing how he or she would make the same submission in practice.

● **The social element**

You should ascertain in advance whether the practitioner giving the masterclass is free to stay on afterwards. If so, consider laying on a reception of some sort. It need not be lavish, but it can provide an important opportunity for the practitioner to speak to the students on an informal basis and to clarify one-to-one any specific points that students wish to raise.

LOGISTICS IN THE RUN-UP TO THE MOOT

By this stage, you will have the structure of your competition in place, you will have arranged the dates and locations of the early-round moots, and the contestants will have been suitably enthused by the introductory masterclass that you have provided. You will even have a cadre of willing judges lined up and ready to jump into action. There is still a bit to do before the night of the first moot, however. Three particular tasks are discussed below: creating a communication network; devising a pre-moot timetable; and facilitating the exchange of authorities and skeleton arguments.

▷ 13.37

Creating a communication network

For the first round of a sizeable mooting competition, you might have 100 people or more involved as mooters, judges and court clerks. Before the moots kick off, you therefore need to devise an efficient system of communicating with them and for them to communicate with each other (for example, to exchange skeleton arguments and lists of authorities). Noticeboards are the time-honoured means of conveying information in most institutions. In the electronic age, however, there are more sophisticated options available. In particular, you can produce a group e-mail with all of those involved as recipients. With one click of your mouse, you will then be able to let them know what is happening, where and when. An

▷ 13.38

13.39 ▷   **Table 13.3:**
Pre-moot timetable

Step	Deadline
The organiser sends a group e-mail to all mooters and judges attaching a spreadsheet with the participants' names and contact details, as well as details of the location and timing of each moot.	M(oot)-21 days
The organiser distributes the moot problem to the mooters and judges.	M-14 days
The mooters exchange lists or bundles of the authorities on which they intend to rely and provide copies to the organiser. If required by the competition rules, the mooters also exchange skeleton arguments and provide copies to the organiser for transmission to the judge.	M-2 days

added advantage of compiling a group e-mail is that it will give you a preliminary list of contact details when it comes to arranging judging and gaining other assistance for the following year's competition.

You should also consider constructing an Excel spreadsheet that sets out who is taking part in each moot and lists everyone's contact details. Colour-coding can make the spreadsheet more user-friendly. Having created a spreadsheet, you could disseminate it in hard copy or electronically. The participants should then have all of the information that they need to make contact with each other.

Pre-moot timetable

13.40 ▷   It is essential to devise a timetable that you and the moot participants must adhere to in the build-up to each moot. Although the precise steps contained in any given timetable will vary from competition to competition, each should provide, at the very least, for the distribution of the moot problem (the organiser's responsibility) and the exchange of authorities and skeleton arguments (the mooters' responsibility). The timetable should be provided as early as possible to all those involved. An example timetable is set out in table 13.3.

Exchange of authorities and skeleton arguments

13.41 ▷   The last element of your pre-moot timetable is the deadline by which the mooters must exchange the authorities on which they intend to rely and any skeleton arguments. In order to mimic practice, it is generally desirable for contestants to exchange authorities at the same time as their skeleton arguments. This should give both the judges and the mooters a sufficient opportunity to read the material in detail prior to the moot.

You will need to decide how exchange is going to take place. You might leave it to the mooters to arrange exchange between themselves and to drop off with you one copy of each document for the judge. Alternatively, you may have to act as a post box through which the mooters exchange their authorities and skeleton arguments. Although this latter course will involve more work for you, it is more likely to ensure that both sides adhere to the required timetable.

DAY OF THE MOOT

The role of the moot organiser on the day of the moot is not dissimilar to that of a "front of house" manager in a theatre. You are the public face of the competition and must troubleshoot any problems that arise. At the same time, you cannot dictate the outcome of the proceedings. That is down to the "cast": the mooters and judges. What you can do, however, is ensure that they have the optimum conditions in which to perform.

> 13.42

      The organiser has a number of important tasks to undertake on the day of the moot. Each of them is described briefly below.

Setting up the moot courtroom

As described in Ch.8, moot courtrooms are arranged in a particular way that reflects the lay-out of real-life courtrooms. You will need to ensure that the rooms in which your moots take place are set up along similar lines. As well as arranging the tables and chairs, you should give some consideration to the following:

> 13.43

● **Seating for the audience**

You will need to make sure that there are sufficient chairs in the room to accommodate spectators. It can be difficult to gauge the likely size of the audience, although the later rounds inevitably attract greater numbers. It is generally better to have too many chairs than too few. Moots that are "standing room only" (believe it or not, they do occasionally happen) may generate the atmosphere of a high-profile libel trial, but you will not endear yourself to the poor souls who have to remain on their feet for an hour or more. You might also consider printing off copies of the moot problem and making them available to the spectators as they arrive. They should, as a result, find it easier to follow the submissions and engage with the moot.

● **Lecterns**

If possible, you should provide at least one lectern for each moot courtroom. Ideally, you will have one per team so that the mooters are not obliged to pass the lectern to each other between speeches. It is possible to improvise if you are faced with a lectern shortage. You might, for example, provide a despatch box that will give the mooters a reasonable platform for their papers.

● **Water**

It is customary to provide a jug of water and glasses both for the mooters and for the judge. The water may be left untouched, but it can be a godsend if one of the participants develops a hacking cough mid-speech.

● **Notices**

Consider putting a notice on the door of each moot courtroom that identifies the names of the mooters and the judge, as well as the relevant round of the competition. Not only will this help the participants and the spectators to work out where they should be, it may even help you.

Briefing the moot court clerk

13.44 ▶ Since mooting competitions invariably impose limits on the speaking time allotted to each mooter, you need to ensure that someone is charged with keeping track of the length of each mooter's submissions. This need is especially acute when the rules of the competition provide that the speaking time allotted to each mooter is exclusive of time spent dealing with judicial interventions since the watch needs to be stopped and started with considerable regularity. Although judges can take on this role, it is preferable to enlist the services of a student volunteer to act as a court clerk. His or her responsibilities need not be limited to timing the submissions, of course. Court clerks can also act as conduits for the mooters to pass any papers up to the judge (or, rarely, *vice versa*) and can assist in setting up the moot courtroom.

If you do employ the services of court clerks, you should brief them on the day of the moot. You should tell them how to time the mooters' submissions and you should explain any mechanism that you have devised for letting the mooters know how much time they have left. The least intrusive method is probably for the court clerk to display a flash card at various intervals; for example, once when a minute remains and again when time is up. An alternative is to use a buzzer or bell, although the noise involved can throw mooters off their stride.

Meeting the judge before the moot begins

13.45 ▶ Once the judge has arrived, the organiser should have a quick word with him or her. The discussion should cover the following areas in particular:

● **Documents**
The organiser should check that the judge has a copy of the moot problem, the authorities relied on by each team, the parties' skeleton arguments (if any), the competition rules, any criteria for judging and giving feedback, and any briefing note that you distributed in advance of the moot.

● **Timing of submissions**
The organiser should explain how the mooters' submissions will be timed. If a court clerk is going to be employed, it may be sensible to introduce him or her to the judges.

● **Choosing a division of labour**
If there is more than one judge, the organiser might suggest that they divide the labour between them, particularly the tasks of making judicial interventions and jotting down the notes that will form the basis for evaluating the mooters' performances.

● **Questions**
It is always worthwhile asking judges whether they have any questions, particularly regarding issues that commonly arise during moots such as the appropriate time limits for the mooters' submissions and the rules on judicial interventions. Organisers should also mention that they or one of their assistants will be available to advise on any particular points that arise.

Assisting the judge when deliberating

Once the mooters have concluded their submissions, most judges will want to deliberate before announcing a decision. You should generally invite judges to retire to another room. If there is nowhere else to go, at least make sure that any discussion between multiple judges takes place outside the earshot of the competitors and spectators. ▶ 13.46

As a judge begins to deliberate, you should check whether any guidance is required. The most common areas of concern tend to be those identified below.

Separating two closely matched teams

The judge may tell you that the moot was extremely closely fought and that he or she is struggling to distinguish between the teams. In those circumstances, you should suggest that the judge focuses on the key skills identified in the competition rules and in any judging criteria that you have produced. Typically, for example, judges will be asked to give particular weight to the abilities of the mooters to deal effectively with judicial interventions. They might, alternatively, lay particular emphasis on the skeleton arguments or on teamwork. Even in very tight contests, there will be objective ways of distinguishing between the contestants. What the organiser must, of course, avoid is attempting to influence the decision.

Dealing with an unbalanced team

In mooting competitions where the best team goes through, judges will sometimes tell you that one team contained both the outstanding individual mooter and the weakest mooter on show. Who, then, should win?

The only advice that you can give in those circumstances is that the judge must advance the best overall team even if that results in the outstanding individual bowing out of the competition. Judges can, of course, emphasise in their feedback how impressed they were by a particular performance. They should be wary of over-doing it, however, given the implication that the team would have won had the best individual's partner been half-competent.

Dealing with breaches of the rules

Judges sometimes ask what they should do about a team that consists of the better mooters, but commits some breach of the rules (typically speaking for too long). The best counsel for the organiser is generally to tell the judge to award the moot to the best team as long as the other side was not materially prejudiced by the breach of the rules. A team might be sufficiently prejudiced, for example, if its opponents failed to serve a skeleton argument in advance of the moot.

AFTER THE MOOT

As each round of your mooting competition finishes and the dust settles, there are two principal tasks that you should consider undertaking (in addition to breathing a deep sigh of relief). ▶ 13.47

Arranging publicity for the winners

It is always a good idea to publicise the winners of each round of moots. This not only serves to validate the students' efforts, it also increases the profile of the competition. Publicity might ▶ 13.48

take the form of an announcement on noticeboards around the institution or in the student newspaper. You will probably want to engage in more elaborate publicity for the overall winners of the competition. Some institutions will, for example, hang photographs of past winners in the law library. There might even be a short presentation by the dean of the faculty.

Enlisting contestants to help with future competitions

13.49 As one year's competition draws to a close, you should be looking towards next year's event. Two particular questions should be at the forefront of your mind: who will organise the next competition; and who will act as judges? You can go some way towards easing both concerns by recruiting as many as possible of this year's crop of mooters to help organise and judge next year's competition.

In the case of students who are graduating, it is particularly important to retain their details on file, so that you can track them down in future years and ask them to return as judges. There are few things more satisfying for a moot organiser than introducing past graduates of your mooting competition as practitioner judges. For those competitors who are about to graduate, it is a good idea to bombard them fairly early on with requests to act as judges in coming years. It often makes a big difference if you ask people to help when the positive experience of mooting remains fresh in their minds. If you leave it until the start of the next academic year, your judging pool may have developed other interests.

CHAPTER CHECKLIST

13.50
- Choose an appropriate structure for your competition.
- Determine whether the best team or best two individual mooters should win the moot.
- Draft clear rules for your competition.
- Consider obtaining sponsorship for your competition.
- Select and brief your judges. The briefing should focus on:
  - Intervention.
  - Giving judgment.
  - Giving feedback.
- Consider providing a mooting masterclass.
- Organise logistics on the day of the moot.

Selecting and writing moot problems

Choosing the right moot problem is an essential part of organising a moot. Get it right and even the most pedestrian contestants will find good points to make. Get it wrong and the most talented of mooters will struggle.

▶ 14.1

   You have two principal choices when deciding on your moot problem. The first is to select an existing problem and either use it as it is or modify it in some way. The second is to write your own, original moot problem.

USING EXISTING MOOT PROBLEMS

If your mooting competition is well-established, the chances are that your predecessors will have bequeathed you a stock of moot problems. If you are not in this fortunate position or are simply on the look-out for new problems, there are several sources of moot problems in the public domain. In most cases, the authors make it clear that they are happy for their problems to be reproduced.

▶ 14.2

Where to find existing moot problems

There are two principal sources of existing moot problems: textbooks and the internet. This text provides the illustrative problem of *Cecil v Dickens* and an assortment of specimen problems in Ch.15. Kaye and Townley's, *Blackstone's Book of Moots* contains a large number of sample moot problems. It is now more than fifteen years old, however, so you will need to make sure that the law has not changed in any respect that might materially affect the problem that you select.

▶ 14.3

   There are also a number of websites from which you can download sample moot problems. They include *www.mootingnet.org.uk,* and *http://global.oup.com/uk/academic/higher-education/law/mooting/archive/*. Needless to say, you should always carry out your own due diligence before using any publicly-available problem for one of your moots.

Selecting existing moot problems

Not all moot problems are created equal. It is therefore important to have regard to a few basic questions when assessing the suitability of someone else's moot problem for your mooting competition. In particular, you should ask the following questions:

▶ 14.4

● **Does the moot problem offer credible arguments for both sides?**

There are two common situations in which this may not be so. The first is where the moot problem is old and there has been a subsequent change in the law that provides a definitive answer to all or part of the problem. The second is where the problem was poorly drafted in the first place and excessively favoured one side over the other.

● **Will the moot problem involve too much research?**

Research is, of course, an integral part of mooting. But it is important that the depth of research required is not such that the participants are unable to do justice to themselves without spending untold hours in the law library. If that is what happens, your competition may haemorrhage participants. As a general rule of thumb, try to ensure that at least one of the grounds of appeal that the problem raises lies within an area of law that the contestants have already studied as part of the curriculum. This will not prevent the contestants from having to carry out further research, as it is unlikely that they will have covered the point in sufficient depth for mooting purposes, but it does mean that they will be refining their knowledge rather than researching the problem from first principles.

● **Does the problem reflect the stage that the competition has reached?**

For a first round moot, relatively straightforward problems dealing, for example, with offer and acceptance in contract or liability in negligence tend to work best. More esoteric topics, such as nuisance, occupiers' liability or human rights law, may be appropriate in the later stages of the competition. Of course, the difficulty of the problem is not necessarily linked to the area of law with which it is concerned. Some negligence problems, for example, raise exceptionally complicated issues of law and policy.

● **Is the problem realistic?**

There is a view that realism does not matter and that the facts of moot problems can be ludicrously far-fetched. However, many students respond poorly to scenarios that seem to have more in common with the plot of an Ealing comedy than with the sort of cases that actually play out in the courts. You may also cause problems if the names of the fictitious parties are so amusing that they become a distraction at the moot itself. Whilst a degree of unreality is inevitable, it is best to choose problems that are based on factual scenarios that might arise in real life.

Tips for modifying existing moot problems

14.5 ▶ You may find that you like the basic scenario of an existing moot problem, but are not completely satisfied that it meets your requirements. You might then look to modify it. Although the precise modifications that you make will obviously depend on the deficiencies that you perceive in the original problem, there are two particular tweaks that you might consider making:

● **Expanding the findings of fact of the trial judge**

Some moot problems, particularly in the realms of contract and tort/delict, do not make it clear whether the trial judge made a finding on causation. This can leave the contestants free to argue the point, which they often do with mixed results. If you come across a moot problem of this sort, you might wish to add particular findings on causation to avoid the mooters speculating about what the trial judge held.

● Adding a cross-appeal

If the moot problem heavily favours one side, you might add a cross-appeal that leans the other way and thereby makes the problem more evenly balanced. If, for example, you have found a negligence problem in which the trial judge decided that a duty of care arose, but gave judgment for the defendant on the basis that there was no causation and that the loss was too remote, you might add a cross-appeal against the judge's findings on breach of duty.

HOW TO WRITE YOUR OWN MOOT PROBLEMS

Although adopting or modifying an existing moot problem can produce perfectly satisfactory results, there are advantages to writing your own. As well as producing a hard-to-rival sense of intellectual satisfaction, you can tailor the problem to fit the dictates of the participants' curriculum or to highlight particular issues of interest. ▶ **14.6**

There are several starting-points for writing moot problems. Three of them are briefly discussed below.

Using "hot topics" as a starting-point

The most fruitful source of new moot problems tends to be those areas of the law (so-called "hot topics") that are generally acknowledged to be intractable or developing, or that have given rise to conflicting judgments in the higher courts. The following are examples of current "hot topics": ▶ **14.7**

Contract law
- Whether an advertisement amounts to a contractually-binding offer or a mere invitation to treat. The leading case is still *Carlill v Carbolic Smokeball Co.*[1] This is an old favourite and a sample moot problem that deals with this area of the law (*Smith v Designer Fashions Limited*) is contained in Ch.15.
- Breach of contract claims in which the party in breach relies on an exclusion clause. These cases lend themselves to moot problems with two grounds of appeal, the first being whether the exclusion clause was incorporated into the contract and the second whether, if so, it satisfied the statutory test of reasonableness.[2]

Criminal law
- What constitutes "property" and "belonging to another" under s.15(1) of the Theft Act 1968. Does this provision cover, for example, a situation in which someone lies about his address in order to get his child into a school for which he was not, in fact, eligible?

---

[1] [1893] 1 Q.B. 256.
[2] Under the Unfair Contract Terms Act 1977 and/or the European regulation.

● The distinction between mens rea and actus reus. An example of this type of problem that is sometimes employed as an interview scenario for intending law students is the situation where a wife attempts to kill her husband (or vice versa if you prefer) by deliberately poisoning his supper. She mistakenly confuses the poison with harmless white powder and the husband survives the meal. The wife then makes her husband a cup of tea and inadvertently adds the poison, believing it to be sugar. She consequently succeeds in killing him this time, but without meaning to. The "moot point" is whether the jury can properly be directed to convict the wife of murder in circumstances where the actus reus and the mens rea of the offence do not coincide.

Equity and the law of trusts

● The circumstances in which voluntary transactions can be set aside where they are vitiated by mistake. This is the issue raised by the specimen moot problem of *Cavendish v Cavendish* in Ch.15.

EU law

● Whether a state-imposed advertising restriction on a particular product constitutes a "measure having equivalent effect" and, if so, whether the member state can justify it under Art.30 or Art.56 of the EU Treaty. For a consideration of these issues by the European Court of Justice, see case C-405/98 *Konsumentombudsmannen v Gourmet International Products AB*,[3] which concerned Sweden's ban on alcohol advertising.

Land law

● Whether a particular arrangement constitutes a lease or a licence. This is the issue raised by the specimen moot problem of *Jankovic v Petrovic* in Ch.15.
● How to resolve the competing claims of the finder of lost property and the owner of the land on which it was found.

Public law

● The extent to which Art.9 of the ECHR protects every act motivated or inspired by a religion or belief. This issue is dealt with in the specimen moot problem of *Huggins v Hobdell* in Ch.15.
● Whether breach of a particular statute gives rise to an action by an individual for breach of statutory duty.

Scots law

● Whether, if an innocent party purchases property that the seller acquired by fraud, the sale contract is voidable or void.
● Whether it is sufficient in order to establish a defence to a charge of rape for the accused to prove that he genuinely believed that the victim consented or whether he must also show that his belief was based on reasonable grounds.

---

[3] [2001] All ER (EC) 308.

Tort law/delict

- Whether a duty of care in negligence exists to avoid pure economic loss. This is the issue raised by the first ground of appeal in the illustrative problem of *Cecil v Dickens*.
- Whether it is necessary to have a proprietary interest in land in order to found a claim in private nuisance. The specimen moot problem in Ch.15 entitled *Huggins v Hobdell* deals with this issue.
- The circumstances in which a secondary victim can recover damages for nervous shock. A variation on this theme is whether a victim can recover damages for nervous shock after damage to property, say in the aftermath of a burglary.

Using an old seminar or exam question as a starting-point

You may be able to find problem questions that have been used in seminars or exams that, with a little modification, can make effective moot problems. Your primary considerations In hunting for appropriate problem questions are likely to be the subject-matter with which they are concerned and the complexity of the issues that they raise. The best moot problems are generally concerned with mainstream areas of the law and concentrate on a small number of legal issues.

⬤ 14.8

Once you have identified a seminar or exam question that you believe might fit the bill, you should rework it into moot problem format. This is likely to involve the following alterations:

⬤ **Limiting the parties and causes of action**

A moot problem should usually be concerned with a single piece of litigation, not multiple claims involving manifold parties. If the seminar or exam question that you are using addresses numerous claims, rework it to excise all but one.

⬤ **Creating a judgment of the lower court**

Seminar and exam questions normally recite a factual scenario, but not in the form of a judgment. By contrast, a moot problem requires a lower court judgment in order to set up an appeal. However, you can readily turn the factual scenario in a seminar or exam question into the lower court's findings of fact.

⬤ **Drafting the grounds of appeal**

Moot problems need grounds of appeal, which seminar and exam questions rarely have. In most cases, you can simply make the grounds of appeal the opposite of whatever you have stated were the findings of the trial judge. If the judge held, for example, that "the defendant did not provide consideration for the claimant's promise''', the ground of appeal would be that, "the Learned Judge erred in law in finding that the defendant did not provide good consideration for the claimant's promise". Since Scots law does not require consideration, this ground of appeal would plainly not work for a moot north of the Border.

Using an appellate court decision as a starting-point

A further method for drafting moot problems is to find a recent appeal court decision that contains either a dissenting judgment or a judgment in which the judge suggested that, had

⬤ 14.9

the facts been slightly different, he would have reached a contrary conclusion. You can then design a moot problem in which the facts are changed either to raise more starkly the dissenting judge's concerns or specifically to include the facts contemplated by the "differing" judge.

This process can be illustrated briefly by the decision of the House of Lords in *Hunter v Canary Wharf Limited*,[4] which overruled the Court of Appeal in finding that the erection of a tall building that interfered with local residents' television reception did not give the residents an actionable claim in private nuisance. By the time the case reached the House of Lords, it raised two legal issues: whether interference with television reception is capable of constituting an actionable nuisance; and whether it is necessary to have an interest in property to claim in private nuisance. Lord Cooke dissented on the second of these issues (the majority of the House of Lords found that a property interest is a prerequisite of bringing a claim). This second issue accordingly offers scope for use in a moot problem.

If you were to use *Hunter* as the basis for a moot problem, you might end up drafting something that looks a little like *Huggins v Hobdell*, the specimen moot problem contained in Ch. 15. That problem also includes a ground of appeal based on the Human Rights Act 1998. This legislation played no part in *Hunter*, but it is often a useful source of grounds of appeal when drafting moot problems.

CHAPTER CHECKLIST

14.10 ▶
- Selecting an appropriate mooting problem is crucial to the success of the moot.
- If you use an existing moot problem, ensure that it:
  - Offers credible arguments for both sides.
  - Does not require excessive legal research.
  - Reflects the stage of the competition.
- If you write your own moot problem, start from either:
  - A "hot topic".
  - An old seminar/exam question.
  - An appellate court decision.

---

[4]   [1997] A.C. 655.

▶ 15
Original moot problems

Even if you follow the guidance offered in Ch.14, writing moot problems can be a time-consuming business. This chapter therefore contains 10 original moot problems covering six of the core subjects on the undergraduate legal curriculum: contract law, criminal law, equity and trusts, land law, public law and tort law/delict. Some of these moot problems are more challenging than others. Possibly the most difficult is *Huggins v Hobdell*, which is concerned with private nuisance and the European Convention on Human Rights. The three most straight-forward moot problems are *Smith v Designer Fashions Limited* (contract law), *Jankovic v Petrovic* (land law) and *Rosser v Bike Guildshire Limited* (public law). ▶ 15.1

Please feel free to use any of the moot problems contained in this chapter in competitions that you organise. We ask only that you check before doing so that the law has not changed and that the problem accordingly still provides arguable points on both sides.

CONTRACT LAW

Smith v Designer Fashions Limited
This problem is concerned with the formation of contracts, specifically the distinction between binding offers and non-binding invitations to treat, and the terms on which offers are made. ▶ 15.2

IN THE COURT OF APPEAL (CIVIL DIVISION)

Joe Smith

-and-

Designer Fashions Limited

On January 1, 2014, Designer Fashions Limited published an advertisement in the Watford Gazette stating as follows:

> "Want to look sharp in 2014? Then take advantage of this amazing bargain. The first man into our Watford shop on January 2, 2014 gets to buy the Armani suit of his choice for just £10."

Joe Smith saw the advertisement and queued up all night outside Designer Fashions Limited's Watford shop. At 9.15am on January 2, 2014, he was the first customer admitted to the store. He selected a three-button sky blue Armani suit and proceeded to the cash desk. The sales assistant refused to sell the suit to Mr Smith for £10 stating that the promotion was no longer valid because a four-button jet black Armani suit had already been sold to the store's assistant manager, who had entered via a staff entrance at 9.00am.

Mr Smith sued Designer Fashions Limited in the Watford County Court. At first instance, Circuit Judge Pearl held that the advertisement was an invitation to treat rather than a contractual offer. She accordingly found in favour of Designer Fashions Limited and dismissed the claim.

Mr Smith now appeals to the Court of Appeal on the following grounds:

1. The judge erred in law in concluding that the advertisement was an invitation to treat and not an offer.
2. The offer contained an implied term that it was only open to bona fide customers and not to staff who worked at the Designer Fashions Limited store.

Buchanan v Thomas

15.3 ▶ This problem raises two main issues: the circumstances in which contractual offers may be withdrawn, and the circumstances in which a term may be implied into a contract.

IN THE COURT OF APPEAL (CIVIL DIVISION)

Max Buchanan

-and-

Tristan Thomas

Max Buchanan, a well-known radio DJ, announced on his radio show his intention to cycle from London to Edinburgh to raise money that he would then donate to charity. Tristan Thomas, an entrepreneur and CEO of Thomas Enterprises Plc, called into the show. On air, he and Max had the following exchange:

TRISTAN: "Max, I know you are fat and out of shape, so £100,000 says you can't do it within four days."
MAX: "Thanks for this very generous sponsorship, which will give me all the incentive I need to train and ride hard."

A few days later, Max started the ride in London. He cycled on a tandem with his colleague Ginny Bains. Max and Ginny took an hour's break each day to broadcast his show from a back-up bus. When Max and Ginny were passing through Carlisle, Tristan called into the show. He and Max had the following exchange:

TRISTAN: "Max, you fraud, the challenge is off because my offer to you was on the assumption that you would cover the whole distance yourself."

MAX: "I'm sorry old chap. The deal is done and you will owe me by the time I reach Edinburgh."

Max and Ginny cycled into Edinburgh within four days of leaving London. When Tristan subsequently refused to pay Max the sum of £100,000, Max sued him for it in the High Court.
At first instance, Chasterton J dismissed the claim on the following basis:

(i) There was no binding contract between Max and Tristan because Tristan was entitled to withdraw his offer at any time before Max arrived in Edinburgh and did so.

(ii) If contrary to finding (i) there was a binding contract, it was not a term of the contract that Max had to cycle the whole distance on his own and he therefore did not breach the contract by riding on a tandem.

Max now appeals to the Court of Appeal on the following ground:
There was a binding contract because once Max accepted the offer during the first on-air conversation with Tristan, he could not withdraw it.
Tristan cross appeals on the basis that, if Max succeeds on his appeal and there was a binding contract, Max breached the contract by riding on a tandem as it was a term of the contract that Max had to cycle the whole distance on his own.

CRIMINAL LAW

R v Hanson

This problem is concerned with certain elements of the offence of kidnap.

▶ 15.4

IN THE COURT OF APPEAL (CRIMINAL DIVISION)

R

-and-

Julia Hanson

Julia Hanson retained Frost & Partners, a firm of solicitors, to act for her in the purchase of a holiday flat in Devon. Ms Hanson believed that she had agreed with Sarah Frost, the senior partner of Frost & Partners, that Frost & Partners would do the work for £300 plus VAT. After the transaction was completed, however, Ms Hanson received a bill for £600 plus VAT. She refused to pay it.
A few weeks later, Ms Hanson asked Ms Frost in writing to send her the conveyancing file for the purchase. Ms Hanson was dissatisfied with the work of the surveyor who advised her. She wanted to review the file to assess whether she could bring a claim in negligence against the surveyor. Ms Frost responded by letter stating that she was exercising a lien over the file and would not release it until her firm's costs were paid in full.

Two days after she received the letter, Ms Hanson e-mailed Ms Frost. The email said that Ms Hanson wanted Ms Frost to provide some tax advice but that, as the matter was complex, it would be necessary to meet face to face. Ms Frost responded by email, suggesting a meeting at her offices the following week. Ms Hanson agreed.

The meeting duly started in a conference room at the offices of Frost & Partners. After a short preliminary discussion about her tax affairs, Ms Hanson suggested adjourning to Ms Frost's office because there were several documents there relevant to Ms Hanson's tax affairs. Ms Frost agreed. On entering Ms Frost's office, Ms Hanson announced that she would not leave it unless she was given her conveyancing file. Ms Frost refused. Ms Hanson became increasingly agitated and Ms Frost, fearing that Ms Hanson might assault her, hit the panic button under her desk. Two security guards arrived, who escorted Ms Hanson from the premises.

A few months later, Ms Hanson was prosecuted in the Crown Court for kidnap. At trial, Owen J directed the jury as follows:

> If the jury was satisfied that Ms Hanson's intention in requesting a meeting with Ms Frost was to force Ms Frost to hand over the conveyancing file against her will, the jury was entitled to find that Ms Hanson "took Ms Frost away by fraud without Ms Frost's consent" even though Ms Hanson asked for the meeting to discuss a bona fide transaction.

The jury convicted Ms Hanson. She now appeals on the grounds that the learned judge erred in law as follows:

There cannot be a kidnap in circumstances where the "victim" agreed to the meeting, suggested that the meeting take place in her firm's offices, and was not taken anywhere.

R v Hesketh

15.5 ▷ This problem deals with certain elements of the offence of handling stolen goods under s.22 of the Theft Act 1968.

IN THE COURT OF APPEAL (CRIMINAL DIVISION)

R

-and-

Robert Hesketh

Robert Hesketh was tried at High Wycombe Crown Court for the offence of handling stolen goods pursuant to section 22 of the Theft Act 1968. At trial, the prosecution and defence agreed the following facts:

(A) Mr Hesketh paid £500 in cash for a Naim Supernait amplifier to a man he knew as Darren who ran a stall selling bric-a-brac at Chesham market.

(B) The list price of a new amplifier was £2,500.

(C) Darren told Mr Hesketh that the amplifier was new, but had been used as a demonstration model.

(D) Darren supplied the amplifier to Mr Hesketh without packaging or any form of guarantee.

(E) At the time of the transaction, there were reports in the local media of a recent break-in at Roberts Hi-Fi shop in High Wycombe.

(F) The amplifier had, in fact, been stolen from Roberts Hi-Fi shop during the break-in.

Mr Hesketh testified at his trial that he did not believe that the amplifier was stolen property. He said that one of his character traits was that he took people at face value. He thought Darren had an honest face and was a bona fide market trader who had come by the amplifier legitimately. Mr Hesketh also said that he and Darren had an amicable ten-minute conversation prior to the transaction during which Darren talked knowledgeably about different models of amplifier.

The judge gave the following directions to the jury at Mr Hesketh's trial:

(i) The jury was entitled to convict Mr Hesketh if it determined that he believed it was "virtually certain" that the amplifier had been stolen.

(ii) For these purposes, the jury was entitled to assume that Mr Hesketh believed what a reasonable man with his characteristics and knowledge at the time of the alleged offence would have believed.

Mr Hesketh was convicted. He now appeals to the Court of Appeal on the grounds that a defendant cannot properly be convicted of handling stolen goods pursuant to section 22 of the Theft Act 1968 unless the jury is directed as follows:

1. It must be satisfied that the defendant was "certain" that the goods were stolen.
2. In determining the defendant's state of mind, it must have regard to his actual belief, not to what a reasonable man in the defendant's position would have believed.

EQUITY AND TRUSTS

Cavendish v Cavendish

This problem concerns the circumstances in which a voluntary disposition under a will may be ▶ 15.6 set aside on the grounds of mistake. It also raises as an issue the scope of the change of position defence.

IN THE COURT OF APPEAL (CIVIL DIVISION)

John Cavendish

-and-

Owen Cavendish

John Cavendish, a 60-year-old retired garage owner, lives in and owns the freehold of 'Badgerslair', a large townhouse in Palmers Green, North London. There is no mortgage over the property. In August 2014, Mr Cavendish consulted his friend, Peter Kenneth, an independent financial adviser, about leaving the property to Owen Cavendish, Mr Cavendish's nephew, only living relative and the main beneficiary under his will. Mr Cavendish wanted to know whether he could ensure that Owen inherited the house in such a way that inheritance tax was not payable on it and he (John) could continue to live in it for as long as he wished.

Mr Kenneth advised that, if Mr Cavendish gifted the house to Owen, inheritance tax would not be due on it provided Mr Cavendish survived for seven years from the date of the gift. Mr Kenneth also explained that Mr Cavendish could continue to live in the house and that, if he wanted security of tenure, Owen could grant him a licence to remain there.

In reliance on this advice, in September 2014, Mr Cavendish conveyed 'Badgerslair' to Owen by a deed of gift and Owen granted Mr Cavendish a licence.

In November 2014, Mr Cavendish mentioned the deed of gift and licence to Steve Cummings, his accountant. Mr Cummings told Mr Cavendish that, regardless of the deed of gift, the house would be included in Mr Cavendish's estate for inheritance tax purposes because there had been a reservation of benefit within the meaning of s.102 of the Finance Act 1986. He also explained that Owen could revoke the licence at any time, potentially making Mr Cavendish homeless.

On receiving this advice, Mr Cavendish asked Owen whether he would agree to set the gift aside. Owen refused to do so, saying that he had recently given up his job as an IT consultant in order to retrain as a teacher in expectation of being able to raise a loan secured on 'Badgerslair' to tide him over financially.

Mr Cavendish accordingly applied to the court for an order that the deed of gift be set aside pursuant to the court's equitable jurisdiction to grant relief for mistaken voluntary dispositions. At first instance, Hildegard J dismissed the claim on the following basis:

(i) The court may only set aside a voluntary disposition if the disponor is mistaken as to the effect of the disposition rather than its financial consequences. That was not the case here.

(ii) Even if the Court were satisfied that there was a mistake as to the effect of the disposition, it would deny the relief sought because Owen had changed his position in reliance on the disposition.

In reaching his decision, the judge made the following findings of fact:

(A) The gift of the house would not achieve an inheritance tax saving if Mr Cavendish continued to occupy it and Owen could revoke the licence at will. Mr Kenneth's advice had therefore been wrong.

(B) Mr Kenneth was now insolvent and did not have any professional indemnity insurance cover.

(C) Although Owen's decision to requalify as a teacher was motivated by the fact that, as the freehold owner of 'Badgerslair', he would be able to fund his studies by raising a mortgage over the property, it could not be said that, but for the gift, he would not have made this decision because he might have been able to raise the necessary finance by other means.

Mr Cavendish now appeals to the Court of Appeal on the basis that the learned judge erred in law in the following respects:

1. The relief sought is available not only when a disponor makes a mistake about the effect of a transaction, but when the disponor makes other mistakes of sufficient seriousness, as occurred in this case.
2. The defence of change of position is only available if it can be demonstrated that the change of position was caused wholly by the mistaken transfer. It was not in this case.

LAND LAW

Jankovic v Petrovic
This problem is concerned with the distinction between a lease and a licence. ▶ 15.7

IN THE COURT OF APPEAL (CIVIL DIVISION)

Janna Jankovic

-and-

Victor Petrovic

Victor Petrovic is a wealthy businessman who was born and raised in Belgrade. Since 2000, he has let the basement flat in his Mayfair townhouse to junior doctors who also hail from Serbia. The flat has its own access directly onto the street and a lockable door that leads into Mr Petrovic's kitchen.

In early July 2013, Mr Petrovic entered into a contract with Dr Janna Jankovic regarding his basement flat. The contract was described on its face as a "licence agreement" and its key terms were as follows:

(a) Dr Jankovic could occupy the flat for one year starting on August 1, 2013 at a rent of £600 per month.
(b) Mr Petrovic or his agents would not enter the flat during the period of Dr Jankovic's occupation except that his cleaner could come into the flat on a weekly basis and his handyman could do so on an occasional basis. Both the cleaner and the handyman would enter the flat via the connecting door from Mr Petrovic's kitchen.
(c) Mr Petrovic was entitled to enter into an agreement in identical terms with a second person who would share the flat with Dr Jankovic. In that event, Dr Jankovic's rent would immediately be reduced to £300 per month.

When the one-year period expired on July 31, 2014, Dr Jankovic refused to move out of the flat and claimed that the arrangement between her and Mr Petrovic constituted a tenancy. When Mr Petrovic rejected Dr Jankovic's assertion, she sought declaratory relief in the High Court.

At first instance, Parker J found, applying *Street v Mountford* [1985] AC 809, that Dr Jankovic was a licencee and not a tenant. In reaching her decision, the judge made the following findings of fact:

(A) Mr Petrovic intended to provide short-term subsidised accommodation for young Serbian doctors to allow them to find their feet in London. He envisaged that they would then move on to other accommodation. He did not intend to give them any of the rights a tenant would enjoy.

(B) The open-market rent for the basement flat was approximately £800 per week during the period August 1, 2013 to July 31, 2014.

(C) Mr Petrovic's cleaner and handyman only visited the flat once each between August 1, 2013 and July 31, 2014 because Dr Jankovic made it clear that she preferred to do the cleaning and any necessary DIY herself.

(D) At all times, Dr Jankovic lived in the flat alone.

Dr Jankovic now appeals to the Court of Appeal on the basis that the judge erred in law in concluding that she was a licencee and not a tenant.

PUBLIC LAW

Rosser v Bike Guildshire Limited

15.8 This problem deals with the meaning of the term "public authority" under the Human Rights Act 1998.

<u>IN THE COURT OF APPEAL (CIVIL DIVISION)</u>

Pauline Rosser

-and-

Bike Guildshire Limited

In January 2014, Guildshire County Council ("the Council") decided to establish a company, Bike Guildshire Limited ("BGL"), to promote cycling within the county. BGL has one member of staff, Lisa Scott, a former council employee. BGL employs her on a one-year fixed-term contract. BGL pays Ms Scott with seed money from the Council and she works from an office in a Council building in Guildshire. The Council's intention was that BGL would become financially self-sufficient within one year of its establishment as a result of revenue generated by advertising space on a "Cycle Guildshire" website administered by BGL.

In March 2014, Ms Scott decided to create a "Bike Hero" award for businesses within

the county that were able to demonstrate that they met the needs of cyclists. She published details of the scheme—including the criteria for receiving the award and instructions on how businesses should apply—on the "Cycle Guildshire" website. The website stated that all applications for "Bike Hero" status would be determined exclusively by BGL.

In April 2014, Pauline Rosser, who is the proprietor of the "Rose Cottage" bed and breakfast in Asheridge Forest, Guildshire, applied to BGL for "Bike Hero" status for her bed and breakfast. Ms Scott refused the application on the basis that "Rose Cottage" did not have enough secure bicycle storage. Shortly afterwards, Ms Rosser discovered that, during the week when her application for "Bike Hero" status was rejected, an application by Ms Scott's boyfriend, Gary Fisher, was successful. He was granted "Bike Hero" status for "Spoke House", another bed and breakfast in Asheridge Forest.

Ms Rosser sued BGL for loss of profit that she claimed resulted from a significant decline in bookings from cycle tourists after April 2014. She claimed that potential customers chose not to stay at "Rose Cottage" because it did not have "Bike Hero" status. Ms Rosser alleged that Ms Scott was obviously biased because her boyfriend owns a competing bed and breakfast in Asheridge Forest and that Ms Rosser's right to a fair trial under Art.6 the European Convention on Human Rights had been infringed.

At first instance, Condor J dismissed the claim on the basis that BGL was not a "public authority" within the meaning of the Human Rights Act 1998 ("the Act").

Ms Rosser now appeals to the Court of Appeal on the ground that BGL was a "public authority" within the meaning of the Act.

TORT LAW/DELICT

Huggins v Hobdell

This problem is concerned with the *locus standi* of claimants to bring actions in private nuisance. It also raises a public law issue regarding the application of Art.9 of the European Convention on Human Rights.

▶ 15.9

IN THE COURT OF APPEAL (CIVIL DIVISION)

(1) Daniel Huggins

(2) Sarah Huggins

-and-

Jeffrey Hobdell

Daniel and Sarah Huggins, who are brother and sister and both in their 20s, live in their parents' house, 78 Orslow Gardens, London ("the Property"). Their parents own the Property jointly. At all material times, their parents lived and worked in Saudi Arabia, only returning to the Property for a week each Christmas.

Jeffrey Hobdell recently bought and moved into the next-door property, 80 Orslow

Gardens. Mr Hobdell is a member of a pagan cult that worships the sun. In that capacity, he meets with as many as 10 other followers of the cult in his garden at sunrise every day, when they mark the sunrise with a 30-minute service that consists of chanting and letting off fireworks.

The Hugginses find that this ceremony interrupts their sleep, particularly in the summer. After making a series of complaints to Mr Hobdell, they commenced proceedings against him in the High Court alleging that the cult's activities constitute a private nuisance and seeking an injunction to restrain Mr Hobdell from engaging in chanting or letting off fireworks.

At the trial of the claim, Mr Justice Rymon made the following findings of fact:

(A) Both the chanting and the fireworks were clearly audible from the Huggins's bedrooms notwithstanding that the windows were double-glazed.
(B) The Hugginses were in no physical danger from the fireworks.
(C) Paganism does not require Mr Hobdell to chant or let off fireworks because it prescribes no single method of celebrating sunrise, but merely requires "worship of the sun and moon".
(D) Mr Hobdell's sole motivation for his behaviour was his pagan belief that the sunrise should be marked.

Mr Justice Rymon refused the injunction on the following grounds:

(i) Since the Hugginses had no proprietary interest in the Property, being bare licensees, they had no legal right to bring a claim for private nuisance.
(ii) Neither chanting nor letting off fireworks constituted an act of nuisance in this context.
(iii) Even if the Hugginses had a claim in private nuisance, it was subject to Mr Hobdell's right under Art.9 of the European Convention on Human Rights ("the ECHR") to manifest his religion or beliefs.

The Hugginses now appeal to the Court of Appeal on the following grounds:

1. The judge erred in law in finding that it is necessary to have a proprietary interest in property in order to found a claim in private nuisance.
2. The judge erred in law in finding that Article 9 of the ECHR applies in circumstances where Mr Hobdell's actions were not required by but simply motivated by his religious beliefs.

Patel v Mills t/a "Executive Lunches"

15.10 ▶ This problem concerns the existence of duties of care in negligence and remoteness of damage.

IN THE COURT OF APPEAL (CIVIL DIVISION)

Sonia Patel

-and-

Paul Mills trading as "Executive Lunches"

Paul Mills is a sole trader who runs a catering business trading as "Executive Lunches". He contracted with one of his regular clients, Harrison Harman & Sons, a firm of estate agents, to provide lunch for 10 people attending a business conference. Mr Mills and Harrison Harman & Sons agreed that the lunch would consist of a range of sandwiches, salads and desserts.

Mr Mills prepared and delivered the food, which included a Caesar salad. One of the delegates at the conference was Sonia Patel, a freelance property photographer. She is allergic to eggs. She suffered severe anaphylactic shock after she ate the Caesar salad. She was rushed to hospital, where the doctors confirmed that she had reacted to traces of egg yoke in the dressing on the Caesar salad.

Ms Patel made a full recovery, but had to stay in hospital for a week. During this time, she could not complete any of the assignments that she was already booked to undertake that week and lost the opportunity to bid for several other jobs.

Ms Patel sued Mr Mills for damages representing the following heads of loss:

(a) Her pain and suffering.
(b) Her lost earnings from the booked engagements she missed during her week in hospital.
(c) Her lost future earnings from three jobs for which she was unable to bid during her week in hospital.

The trial judge, Nemubla J, made the following findings of fact:

(A) Harrison Harman & Sons did not notify Mr Mills of any special requirements for the food.
(B) Mr Mills only knew that the lunch was for delegates at a business conference. He did not know who would attend.

Nemubla J found for Ms Patel on the basis that Mr Mills owed her a duty of care in negligence to warn her that some of his dishes were unsuitable for people who suffer from certain allergies. On that basis, the judge awarded Ms Patel damages of £1,500 for her lost earnings on booked assignments and £3,000 for her lost future earnings on contracts for which she was unable to bid.

Mr Mills now appeals to the Court of Appeal on the following grounds:

1. He owed no duty of care to notify the delegates at the conference that some of his dishes were unsuitable for sufferers of certain allergies, particularly because

his customer, Harrison Harman & Sons, did not raise any concerns with him about allergies.

2. Even if Mr Mills owed a duty of care to Ms Patel, her claim for £3,000 for lost future earnings was not recoverable in law because it was too remote.

Pendleton v Cali Cleaning Services

15.11 This problem is concerned with the existence of duties of care in negligence and remoteness of damage.

IN THE COURT OF APPEAL (CIVIL DIVISION)

Emma Pendleton

-and-

Cali Cleaning Services

Cali Cleaning Services ("Cali") is a specialist office cleaning company. It has a contract to provide cleaning services to the London College of Advocacy and Communication Skills ("the College"). Emma Pendleton is a self-employed lecturer who provides specialist advocacy training to the College and other clients.

Ms Pendleton taught a two-day course at the College on June 15 and 16, 2014. Because she cycled to work, she left her Armani work suit and a silver necklace in the College's staff room overnight on June 15, 2014.

After Ms Pendleton left work on the evening of June 15, 2014, the College was cleaned by employees of Cali. One of them was Kristian Lopez. He was the last person to leave the College. When he did so, late at night, he forgot to lock the side door to the building, which gave access onto a public street. Kristian quickly realised his mistake and returned to the College 10 minutes later to lock the side door. Unfortunately, during that time an intruder had entered the College through the unlocked door and had stolen several items belonging to the College together with Ms Pendleton's suit and necklace.

Ms Pendleton sued Cali for negligence, claiming damages representing the replacement cost of her suit and necklace. The judge at first instance, Quealy J, made the following findings of fact:

(A) Mr Lopez knew Ms Pendleton well as they often chatted in the staff room together, but he wrongly assumed that she was a College employee.

(B) Mr Lopez knew that Ms Pendleton cycled to work every day because he had often seen her in her cycling kit arriving at and leaving the College.

Quealy J dismissed Ms Pendleton's claim on the following basis:

(i) Cali owed no duty of care to Ms Pendleton because she was self-employed and not an employee of the College.

(ii) Even if a duty of care arose, the loss Ms Pendleton suffered was irrecoverable because it was not foreseeable that valuable items of personal clothing and jewellery would be left unsecured at the College overnight.

Ms Pendleton now appeals to the Court of Appeal on the following grounds:

1. Cali owed her a duty of care in negligence to take reasonable care and skill when cleaning the College.
2. Her losses are recoverable and not too remote.

Appendices

APPENDIX I
Specimen mooting competition rules

These specimen rules contain a number of optional provisions that have been inserted in A1.1 square brackets.

RULES OF [INSERT INSTITUTION] MOOTING COMPETITION [INSERT DATE]

1. In these Rules, the "Organiser" is defined as [insert name of organiser] or his designated representative.
2. The competition shall be open to teams of two students both of whom shall be studying the [insert name of course] as of [insert date].
3. [The Organiser will hold a draw to determine the members of each team. Once drawn, team members may not be changed from round to round except with the express written permission of the Organiser, which will only be given in exceptional circumstances.]
4. The competition shall be run on a ["knockout"/"Champions League"] basis with each round taking place on the date advertised in the mooting brochure, copies of which are available from the Organiser.
5. A moot may only be rescheduled with the express permission of the Organiser, which shall only be given in exceptional circumstances.
6. The Organiser will hold a draw to determine the teams that will compete against each other at each moot.
7. Each moot will have one judge except for the final of the competition, which will be presided over by three judges.
8. The Organiser will distribute the moot problem for each round to all mooters involved by e-mail two weeks before the round is due to take place. At the same time, the Organiser will advise each team whether it represents the [appellant/reclaimer] or the respondent.
9. The Organiser will keep a chart on his or her office door showing the progress of the competition and the result of each moot.
10. Any apparent ambiguity arising out of a moot problem shall be brought to the attention of the Organiser within three days of receipt of the problem by the teams in accordance with rule 8 above. The Organiser shall have absolute discretion to resolve the ambiguity.

11. Each team will be entitled to rely at the moot on a maximum of three authorities, i.e. reported cases, institutional writers, textbooks and journal articles. Extracts from authorities contained in any authority relied on by a team shall not constitute additional authorities for these purposes. By no later than 5pm two working days before the moot is scheduled to take place, each team must supply to the other team and to the Organiser a written list of the authorities on which it will rely at the moot.

12. [Each team must prepare a skeleton argument, which should not exceed two sheets of A4 paper, that sets out the main points of its argument and includes citations and page references for each authority on which it relies. By no later than 5pm two working days before the moot is scheduled to take place, each team will supply a copy of its skeleton argument to the other team and to the Organiser by e-mail. The judge may at his or her absolute discretion refuse to hear an argument that has not been raised in outline in a team's skeleton argument or may take the omission from the skeleton argument into account in deciding which team should win the moot.]

13. Each moot will start promptly at the starting time advised by the Organiser. If any contestant is late, the judge may decide in his or her absolute discretion to start the moot in the contestant's absence and take lateness into account in deciding which team should win the moot.

14. [At the start of the moot, each team must provide the judge with a bundle containing full unmarked photocopies or print-offs of each authority on which it will rely at the moot.]

15. Each participant shall be permitted to speak at the moot for a maximum of 10 minutes, [save that the team representing the appellant will be allowed an additional five minutes in which to reply to the respondent's case]. Time taken up in making and responding to judicial interventions will not count towards these time limits.

16. The order of speeches at the moot will be as follows: [in England and Wales: leading counsel for the appellant, junior counsel for the appellant, leading counsel for the respondent, junior counsel for the respondent and leading counsel for the appellant in reply; in Scotland: junior counsel for the appellant/reclaimer, junior counsel for the respondent, senior counsel for the appellant/reclaimer and senior counsel for the respondent].

17. At the end of the moot, the judge shall give judgment as follows: (1) an adjudication on the points of law raised in the moot and (2) a decision as to which team has won the moot, including any feedback on the participants' performances. In reaching a decision as to which team has won the moot, the judge shall take into account each of the overriding, general and specific criteria listed below.

18. There shall be no appeal against the judge's judgment.

19. Any objection to the outcome of a moot, which may only be based on an alleged infringement of these Rules, shall be made to the Organiser in writing by no later than 5pm on the day following the moot. The Organiser's decision on the objection will be final.

20. The Organiser shall have absolute discretion to amend these Rules and to resolve any question concerning their interpretation.

CRITERIA FOR DETERMINING THE WINNER OF EACH MOOT

The criteria set out below are accompanied, where appropriate, by explanatory notes in italics.

<u>Overriding Criterion</u>

- Be persuasive.

The judge will allocate approximately 10% of the overall marks to this criterion.

<u>General Criteria</u>

- Speak at appropriate pace and volume.
- Be concise and use plain English.
- Structure submissions in a logical manner.
- Demonstrate appropriate manners and etiquette.

Mooters must be courteous to judges and opponents alike, and ensure that they are correctly attired for a moot courtroom.

- Deal effectively with judicial interventions.
- Work as a team.
- Abide by the rules of the competition.

Mooters should bear in mind, in particular, the obligations to exchange lists of authorities [and skeleton arguments] timeously and to keep their submissions within the time limits allowed.

The judge will allocate approximately 40% of the overall marks to these criteria.

<u>Specific Criteria</u>

- Effectively outline the issue/s and how you propose to deal with them.
- Introduce and use authorities effectively, distinguishing where necessary.

Mooters should explain how each authority relates to the submission being made, ask whether the judge has read the authority and make it clear which passages are relied on.

- [Refer to and expand upon the arguments put forward in your skeleton argument.

Mooters are not allowed to run arguments that are not identified in their skeleton argument.]

- Make effective submissions that support your case.
- Accurately apply the law to the facts set out in the moot problem.
- Respond to and undermine your opponents' arguments.

The judge will allocate approximately 50% of the overall marks to these criteria.

▶ APPENDIX II
Specimen judge's score sheet

A2.1▶ The score sheet set out below is based on the criteria that appear in the specimen mooting competition rules at Appendix II

Appellant

Name of mooter	Overriding criterion (10%)	General criteria (40%)	Specific criteria (50%)	Total	Comments
Overall team score					

Respondent

Name of mooter	Overriding criterion (10%)	General criteria (40%)	Specific criteria (50%)	Total	Comments
Overall team score					

▶ APPENDIX III
Sample text for freshers' fair brochure

THE [INSERT NAME OF INSTITUTION] MOOTING COMPETITION [INSERT DATE]   ▶ A3.1

This brochure gives a brief description of what a moot is and when the competition will take place. If you are interested in taking part, you will need to attend the introductory lecture on [insert date], at which more details will be provided.

What is a moot?

A moot is a form of legal argument. Two teams, each comprised of two students, are presented with a hypothetical legal problem. Each team must argue one side of the case before a judge or panel of judges. Both team members are obliged to speak, although it is up to them how they divide up the task. At the conclusion of the moot, the judge(s) will deliver judgment on the legal issues and decide which team has won the moot.

An example of a moot

The moot problem might describe a situation like this: party A bought goods from party B and has sued party B for damages because, A alleges, the goods were not of satisfactory quality; party A succeeded in its claim in front of the first instance court and party B is appealing against this decision on the basis that the loss is too remote. In this scenario, one team of mooters would act for party B (the appellant) and argue that the loss is too remote. The other team would act for party A (the respondent) and argue that the loss is not too remote. In order to construct their arguments, both teams would need to research the law on damages and remoteness, and look up any relevant legal authorities.

Competition dates

Out of fairness to all participants, every moot in any given round of the competition will take place on the same night. The dates for each round of moots are as follows:

Round one: [insert date and time]

Quarter-finals: [insert date and time]

Semi-finals: [insert date and time]

Final: [insert date and time]

Each moot will last for approximately one hour and refreshments will be available afterwards.

The sponsor

The competition is sponsored by [insert name of the sponsor], who have kindly provided a prize of [describe prize] to the winning team. The sponsor will also provide judges for the semi-finals and final, and will lead a mooting masterclass on [insert date].

Next steps

If you are interested in taking part in the competition, please give your name to [insert the name of the organiser]. You can contact him by e-mail at [insert e-mail address].

PLEASE NOTE THAT WE ARE UNABLE TO ACCOMMODATE MORE THAN 64 ENTRANTS (32 TEAMS OF 2). IN THE EVENT THAT MORE THAN 64 PEOPLE EXPRESS INTEREST, NAMES WILL BE PULLED OUT OF A HAT TO DETERMINE WHO TAKES PART. IF YOU APPLY AND ARE UNSUCCESSFUL, YOU SHOULD BE AWARE THAT AD HOC MOOTS WILL BE ARRANGED SO THAT YOU HAVE AN OPPORTUNITY TO MOOT DURING THE ACADEMIC YEAR.

APPENDIX IV
Sample text for judge's guidance note

1. The organiser of the competition is [insert name]. At least one week before the moot that you will be judging, [he/she] will advise you of the venue of the moot and will provide you with a copy of the moot problem and a schedule containing the names of the mooters who will be speaking. Please take time to read the moot problem in advance of the moot and, if possible, to think about the points that you would expect both sides to make. If you will be one of a number of judges, please try to discuss the moot problem with your fellow judges before the moot.

2. Approximately two days before the moot takes place, the organiser will send to you copies of the participants' [skeleton arguments and] lists of authorities. Please endeavour to read them before the moot.

3. Unless you are told otherwise by the organiser, the moot will start promptly at 5.30pm. If this is going to be a problem for you, please let the organiser know as soon as possible.

4. You are responsible for ensuring that the lay-out of the moot courtroom is to your satisfaction. Please therefore try to arrive at least 10 minutes early so that adjustments can be made to the room's lay-out if necessary.

5. Each participant is allowed a maximum of 10 minutes in which to make oral submissions. That period does not include time spent dealing with your questions. Please do your best to ensure that the participants keep to this time limit. You might, for example, give a short warning if 10.5 minutes elapse and then refuse to hear anything further at the 11-minute mark. Whatever method you choose to adopt, please employ it consistently.

6. You are encouraged to make interventions where appropriate during each participant's speech. So far as possible, each participant should be subjected to interventions of similar length and complexity. When asking questions of the participants, please try to test the validity of the submission being made rather than the participant's wider knowledge of the law. If a participant is visibly struggling to answer a question, please encourage him or her to move on to another point.

7. After the participants have completed their oral submissions, the organiser will invite you to retire to another room to consider your decision. Please keep your deliberations relatively brief as we do try to complete each moot within an hour.

8. You are asked to give a short reasoned judgment on the legal issues raised by the moot problem before announcing which team has won the moot. Either before or after giving your decision on the moot, you should briefly provide feedback on the strengths and weaknesses of each participant's performance. When you give feedback, please try to follow these short guidelines:

   (1) focus on a small number of points, perhaps two or three, that will make the greatest difference to the overall standard of the participant's performance;

   (2) begin your feedback by mentioning something that the participant did well; and

   (3) when providing negative feedback, try to give concrete examples and suggest how the mistakes could have been avoided.

9. In deciding which team has won the moot, you must have regard to the criteria set out in the competition rules, a copy of which is provided with this guidance note. Of course, these criteria can never be exhaustive and you will inevitably find yourself making some subjective judgments.

10. There will be refreshments after the moot to which you, the participants and the audience are invited. If a participant asks you for further feedback at this point, by all means give it, but do not feel that you have to justify your decision.

11. If you have any questions, whether prior to the moot or on the night itself, please do not hesitate to contact the organiser at [insert contact details].

Index

LEGAL TAXONOMY
FROM SWEET & MAXWELL

This index has been prepared using Sweet and Maxwell's Legal Taxonomy. Main index entries conform to keywords provided by the Legal Taxonomy except where references to specific documents or non-standard terms (denoted by quotation marks) have been included. These keywords provide a means of identifying similar concepts in other Sweet & Maxwell publications and online services to which keywords from the Legal Taxonomy have been applied. Readers may find some minor differences between terms used in the text and those which appear in the index. Suggestions to sweetandmaxwell.taxonomy@thomson.com.